17 SDGs In Action

aSSIST University Press

AUTHORS

PREFACE 1 Dong-sung Cho
PREFACE 2 Yong-joo Choi

1. Jin-hee Choi
2. Young-kee Kim
3. Jeong-myung Gim
4. Song-hyun Joo
5. Jae-eun Kim
6. Hyo-sook Yim
7. Ho-sang Shin
8. Jong-ouk Park
9. Kyung-geun Lee
10. Tae-yeon Oh
11. Joong-ho Chang
12. Tae-hyun Kim
13. Seul-ah Lee
14. Jong-gye Shin
15. Yeo-chang Youn
16. Dal-ju Mun
17. Jeong-ho Pyo

Published by **aSSIST University Press**

17 SDGs In Action

ISBN 979-11-6282-110-7

Printed in Korea.

PREFACE 1

SDGs are a heaven we create on earth for mankind.

Dong-sung Cho, Chair,
The Institute for Industrial Policy Studies Switzerland (IPSS)

1. Prologue

I recently googled the three words "past," "present," and "future."

For "past" there were about 11,690,000,000 results, for "present" about 12,210,000,000 results, and for "future" about 9,790,000,000 results. The most hits are for "present," while the hits for "past" reached 96% of that level and those for "future" reached 80%. As you might expect, "present" is the most important to us, and "past" is the next most important. "future" came in third, but the fact that it reached 80% of "present" is highly significant: The future is worth looking forward to.

I then divided "future" into "bright future" and "dark future" and googled them again.

Bright future: About 649,000,000 results
Dark future: About 1,610,000,000 results

"Dark future" had nearly 2.5 times more searches than "bright future."

Why is this? Does it mean that the future, which is 80% as important to us as the present, does not feel bright, but dark and gloomy?

2. History of SDGs

As we entered the 21st century, the United Nations, the largest and most authoritative international organizations with 193 member nations, developed measures to overcome humanity's anxiety about a bleak future. As a part of this, leaders from 189 countries gathered at the UN Headquarters in New York in September 2000 to sign the Millennium Declaration, an agreement to achieve the Millennium Development Goals (MDGs) by 2015.

The MDGs consisted of 8 goals and 21 measurable detailed targets. The first of the goals was to end poverty and hunger (1), which mandated halving the absolute poor living at less than $1.25 a day by 2015. The following seven goals were to achieve universal primary education (2), to promote gender equality and empower women (3), to reduce child mortality (4), to improve maternal health (5), to combat HIV/AIDS, malaria, and other diseases (6), to ensure environmental sustainability (7), and to develop a global partnership for development (8). The MDGs were mainly aimed at the people of developing countries in the bottom third of the world's 7 billion people with per capita incomes of less than $1,500. The MDGs, announced by then UN Secretary-General Kofi Annan, continued for 15 years until 2015.

The announcement of the MDGs was an earth-breaking event in the sense that mankind joined forces to fight poverty for the first time in human history. However, in 2015, the target year, 12 of the 17 targets of the MDGs were evaluated as not having been achieved, excluding the 4 detailed targets of developing a global partnership for development (8), which did not have quantitative evaluation criteria. In particular, the employment rate (1.b) fell from 62% to 60%. Sustainable development (7.A) was also found to have regressed from before <Table 1>.

Table 1. Millennium Development Goals: Target and Achievement[1]

Did we achieve the Millennium Development Goals (MDGs)?

Summary of global progress of the United Nations' (UN) Millennium Development Goals (MDGs), which spanned the period 2000-2015. Shown are the Targets of the MDGS*, levels in the baseline year, the final target level and actual achieved level for each Target.

- Achieved Targets are marked in **green**;
- Missed Targets are marked in **red.**

Millennium Development Goal(MDG) Target	Baseline level	Target level	Achieved final level
MDG1.A: halve shard of people living in extreme poverty(<$1.25 per day)	47% in developing regions	Reduce to 23.5%	Fell to 14%
MDG1.B: achieve full and productive employment, as well as decent work for all, including young people and women	62% global working-age population in employment	Full(100%)	Fell to 60%
MDG1.C: halve the proportion of individuals suffering from hunger	23.3% in developing regions	Reduce to 11.5%	Fell to 12.9%
MDG2.A: ensure that children universally-including both boys and girls-will be able to complete a full course of primary education	83% in developing regions	Universal(100%)	Increased to 91%
MDG3.A: eliminate gender disparity at all education levels	Developing regions: 0.87 in primary 0.77 in secondary 0.71 in tertiary	Gender parity index(GPI) between 0.97-1.03	Developing regions: 0.98 in primary 0.98 in secondary 1.01 in tertiary
MDG4.A: reduce the under-five mortality rate by two-thirds	90 per 1,000 live births	Reduce to 30 per 1,000	Fell to 43 per 1,000
MDG5.A: reduce the matiernal mortality ration by 75 percent	380 per 100,000 live births	Reduce to 95 per 100,000	Fell to 210 per 1,0000
MDG5.B: achieve universal access to reproductive health.	35% in developing regions	Universal(100%)	Increased to 52%

Millennium Development Goal(MDG) Target	Baseline level	Target level	Achieved final level
Pregnant women receiving adequate antenatal care visits			
MDG5.B: achieve universal access to reproductive health. *Women aged 15-49 in marriage/union, using contraceptives*	55% in developing regions	Universal(100%)	Increased to 64%
MDG6.B: halt and have started to reverse the spread of HIV/AIDS	3.5M new cases per year	0 new cases	2.1M new cases per year
MDG6.B: achieve global access to treatment for HIV/AIDS for those who nees it by 2010	3% of people with HIV	100% of people with HIV	23% of people with HIV (2010) 45% of people with HIV (2015)
MDG6.C: ceased & startes reversal of incidence of malaria & TB. *Incidence of malaria*	158 new cases per 1,000 at risk	Fewer than 158 new cases per 1,000 at risk	Fell to 94 new cases per 1,000 at risk
MDG6.C: ceased & startes reversal of incidence of malaria & TB. *Incidence of tuberculosis (TB)*	172 new cases per 100,000 people	Fewer than 172 new cases per 10,000 at people	Fell to 142 new cases per 100,000 people
MDG7.A: integrate principles of sustainable development into country policies & reverse loss of environmental reaources			Multiple metrics (nearly all deterioratinh)
MDG7.B: reduce biodiversity loss, achieving, by 2010, a significant reduction in the rate of loss			Red List Index shows continued biodiversity loss
MDG7.C: halve the proportion of the proportion of the population without sustainable access to *safe drinking water*	24% without access to improved water source	Reduce to 12% without access	Fell to 9% without access
MDG7.C: halve the proportion of the proportion of the population without sustainable access to *sanitation*	46% without access to improved sanitation	Reduce to 23% without access	Fell to 32% without access

MDGS(Golbal Partnership) does not have easily quantifiable targets and is therefore not included.
source: United Nations (UN), the MDG Report (2015) & MDG Monitor.
The data visualization is avilable at OurWorldinData.org. There you will find further data on this topic.

UN Secretary-General Ban Ki-moon decided to present new goals that the UN should continue to pursue over the next 15 years, based on the experience of the MDGs.[2] He set out the purpose of creating a set of global goals related to the environmental, political, and economic challenges that people face as humanity. At the United Nations Conference on Sustainable Development, held in Rio de Janeiro, Brazil, 2012, Secretary-General Ban asked UN members to submit new proposals by 2013. At the same time, the UN website received a wide range of proposals from people around the world, under the title "What kind of world do you want?" Secretary-General Entrusted by Secretary-General Ban, Nikhil Seth,[3] the current UNITAR Executive Director, sorted out a huge collection of proposals submitted from all over the world.

The 193-member UN General Assembly adopted the 2030 Sustainable Development Agenda on September 25, 2015, with a set of 17 of Sustainable Development Goals that included (1) no poverty, (2) zero hunger, (3) good health and well-being, (4) quality education, (5) gender equality, (6) clean water and sanitation, (7) affordable and clean energy, (8) decent work and economic growth, (9) industry, innovation and infrastructure, (10) reduced inequalities, (11) sustainable cities and communities, (12) responsible consumption and production, (13) climate action, (14) life below water, (15) life on land, (16) peace, justice, and strong institutions, and (17) partnerships for the goals. Secretary-General Ban Ki-moon hailed the SDGs as a universal, integrated, and transformative vision for a better world.[4]

Table 2. shows the list of the 17 SDGs and the number of targets and indicators for each SDG.

SD Goals, Targets, and Indicators

No.	SD Goals	Targets[5]	Indicators[6]
1	End poverty in all its forms everywhere	5+2	10+3
2	End hunger, achieve food security and improved nutrition and promote sustainable agriculture	5+3	10+4
3	Ensure healthy lives and promote well-being for all at all ages	9+4	21+7
4	Ensure inclusive and equitable quality education and promote lifelong learning opportunities for all	7+3	9+3
5	Achieve gender equality and empower all women and girls	6+3	10+4
6	Ensure availability and sustainable management of water and sanitation for all	6+2	9+2
7	Ensure access to affordable, reliable, sustainable and modern energy for all	3+2	4+2
8	Promote sustained, inclusive and sustainable economic growth, full and productive employment and decent work for all	10+2	14+2
9	Build resilient infrastructure, promote inclusive and sustainable industrialization and foster innovation	5+3	9+3
10	Reduce inequality within and among countries	7+3	11+3
11	Make cities and human settlements inclusive, safe, resilient and sustainable	7+3	12+3+(1)
12	Ensure sustainable consumption and production patterns	8+3	10+3
13	Take urgent action to combat climate change and its impacts	3+2	6+2
14	Conserve and sustainably use the oceans, seas and marine resources for sustainable development	7+3	7+3
15	Protect, restore and promote sustainable use of terrestrial ecosystems, sustainably manage forests, combat desertification, and halt and reverse land	9+3	11+3

No.	SD Goals	Targets[5]	Indicators[6]
	degradation and halt biodiversity loss		
16	Promote peaceful and inclusive societies for sustainable development, provide access to justice for all and build effective, accountable and inclusive institutions at all levels	10+2	22+2
17	Strengthen the means of implementation and revitalize the Global Partnership for Sustainable Development	19+0	24+0
Sub-total		126+43	199+49+(1)[7]
Total		169	248[8]+(1)

For the purpose of objectively evaluating performance against the 17 goals and 169 targets, the UN General Assembly adopted the quantifiable global indicator framework on July 6th, 2017. Since then, UN Statistical Commission has annually refined and comprehensively reviewed the indicators. As of June 2022, there are 231 global indicators that UN Statistical Commission will review against actual performances on a global basis.[9] This global indicator framework will be complemented by local indicators at the regional and national levels, which will be independently developed by each region and the respective UN Member countries.

Albeit rooted in the MDGs, SDGs differ from MDGs in five ways, as shown in <Table 3>. First, the SDG idea generators are broader. The UN solicited ideas from 193 UN member countries and global citizens at large through the UN website, while the MDGs were produced by a group of experts within the UN. Second, the SDG targets are wider. SDGs include advanced countries as well as the developing countries originally targeted by the MDGs in 2000. Third, the SDG criteria are flexible, allowing each country the freedom to set its own national criteria for achieving the SDGs. Fourth, the scope of the SDGs is more diverse, including economic growth, social inclusion, and the environment, while the MDGs mainly cover social issues. Fifth, as a result of the fourth difference, the SDGs include more goals, targets, and indicators. At the time of its adoption by UN in 2015, the SDGs comprised 17 goals, 169 targets, and 232[10] indicators, compared to the 8 goals, 21 targets, and 63 indicators of the MDGs.

Table 3. Comparison of the MDGs and SDGs

	MDGs	SDGs
Duration	2000-2015	2015-2030
Proposed by	Kofi Annan	Ban Ki-moon
Difference 1: Ideas generated by	Group of experts	193 UN member countries Global citizens at large
Difference 2: Target	Poor developing countries	Whole world
Difference 3: Criteria	Fixed	Flexible (Country-specific)
Difference 4: Scope	Social	Economic, social, environment

There are a couple of specific characteristics of the SDGs. Secretary-General Ban was conscious of justice and accountability in the process of allocating a large funding for humanitarian purposes. The 16th Goal of the SDGs therefore includes these two words in its title "Promote peaceful and inclusive societies for sustainable development, provide access to justice for all and build effective, accountable, and inclusive institutions at all levels." In this way Secretary-General Ban made it clear that the Overseas Development Assistance (ODA) funds for the purpose of achieving the country-specific goals and targets would not pass into the hands of corrupt dictators in developing countries. For the same purpose, the 17th Goal of the SDGs was set to help promote global partnership, as shown in its title, "Strengthen the means of implementation and revitalize the Global Partnership for Sustainable Development." World's leading scientists and statisticians were invited to take part in the process of developing indicators that are logical and operational.

3. The future of the SDGs in research and education

Understandably, SDGs have been fully recognized and utilized within the UN System and by UN family organizations such as UNITAR, UNESCO, and Global Compact. Outside the UN boundary, however, SDGs have not had as much impact. In the business arena in particular, the SDGs are lagging in popularity behind the recent upsurge of Environmental, Social, and Governance (ESG), measures, which have gained worldwide popularity since 2020 through the leadership of CEO Larry Fink of Blackstone. "Across industries, geographies, and company sizes, organizations have been allocating more resources toward improving ESG. More than 90 percent of S&P 500 companies now publish ESG reports in some form, as do approximately 70 percent of Russell 1000 companies."[11] On the other hand, "among the 8,550 companies in the MSCI All Country World Index, for example, only 0.2% of companies were strongly aligned to the UN SDGs."[12]

I believe that ESG may lead to adopting the SDGs at the end of the day. The reasoning is straightforward. ESG is a powerful means for investors like Blackstone to draw the attention of the business community through their vast funds for asset management. Nevertheless, they do not have sophisticated content and criteria with which to convince companies to follow their leadership in ESG.

As shown in <Table 4>, ESG is a basin-like platform on which the content-loaded SDGs can be stacked. SD Goals 6, 7, 13, 14, and 15 have contents that can be categorized under 'Environment,' SD Goals 1, 2, 3, 4, 5, 8, 9, 10, 11, and 12 under 'Society,' and SD Goals 16 and 17 under 'Governance.' Therefore, ESG and the SDGs can be merged into a single entity for corporations to master and follow.

Table 4. The Relationship between ESG and SDGs

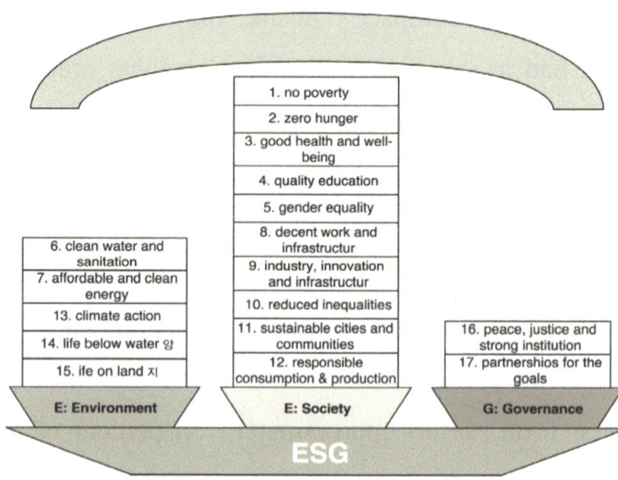

<Table 4> implies that the current movement of ESG may lead to adoption of the SDGs if and when people start to search for content that can fill the three empty basins provided by the ESG movement. In other words, one way to track the progress of ESG is through its alignment with the SDGs. In order to make this happen, we need to conduct research into and learn more about the SDGs in both content and context.

It is in this vein that IPS Switzerland and Franklin University Switzerland have agreed to partner in establishing a new university titled "SDG University." UNITAR has agreed to oversee the establishment and operation of SDG University. The UN Headquarters, with the blessing of Secretary-General Ban Ki-moon, endorsed the use of the term "SDG" as the name of the university.[13]

4. Connecting to the 17 articles

This preface, along with another preface by Co-Rector Choi Yong-ju of SDG University, is followed by 17 articles that explain each of the 17 SDGs in more detail. Together with this preface introducing the history and the future of SDGs, these articles will equip the readers of this book to create a bright future and eventually heaven on earth.

This time I googled the two words "heaven" and "hell." The following numbers appeared:

Heaven: About 1,040,000,000 results
Hell: About 1,170,000,000 results
SDGs About 326,000,000 results

It is a pity that the word "hell" appears more often than the word "heaven." We still have hope. The word "SDGs" returns 326 million hits. Since "SDGs" are a synonym for heaven, "heaven" and "SDGs" together return 1,366 million hits, topping "hell" by a wide margin. Let us put our efforts together to realize the SDGs by 2030, for the SDGs can create a heaven on earth for mankind.

Footnote

1 "Now it is possible to take stock – did the world achieve the Millennium Development Goals?" by Hannah Ritchie and Max Roser, *Our World In Data*, September 20, 2018. https://ourworldindata.org/millennium-development-goals

2 The content of this part was excerpted from my dialogue with UN's 8th Secretary General Ban Ki-moon on December 23rd, 2021, in his office at Ban Ki-moon Foundation in Seoul, Korea.

3 Nikhil Seth was then the Director of the Division for Sustainable Development, Department of Economic and Social Affairs (DESA) at the United Nations Secretariat in New York.

4 "SD in Action," *Newsletter*, UN Sustainable Development Goals Knowledge Platform, Sep. 2015.

5 The first numbers for the Targets show the measurable objectives of mankind, while the second numbers show the measurable resources and regulations that are the means of reaching the objectives.

6 The first numbers for the Indicators show the quantifiable objectives of mankind, while the second numbers show the quantifiable resources and regulations that are the means of reaching the objectives.

7 The parentheses denote the Indicator corresponding to Target 11.c. Although the UN General Assembly adopted 232 global indicators in 2017,the UN Statistical Commission decided not review Target 11.c: "Support least developed countries, including through financial and technical assistance, in building sustainable and resilient buildings utilizing local materials," because "No suitable replacement indicator was proposed."
https://unstats.un.org/sdgs/files/Tier%20Classification%20of%20SDG%20Indicators_9%20Jun%202022_web.pdf

8 Deleting the 17 indicators that are double-counted, the net number of indicators is reduced to 231.

9 https://unstats.un.org/sdgs/iaeg-sdgs/tier-classification/

10 Deleting the indicator for Target 11.c, the net number of Indicators is 231.

11 Sustainability Reporting in Focus, G&A Institute, 2021.

12 "UN Sustainable Development Goals: How Companies Stack Up," Dorothy Neufeld, World Economic Forum, Mar 18, 2021.

13 UN's 8th Secretary General Ban Ki-moon gave his blessings for the inauguration of SDGs University on December 23rd, 2021 in his office at Ban Ki-moon Foundation in Seoul, Korea. Vice President Choi Yong-ju and International Director Kim Kyung-ju of aSSIST University was also present.

PREFACE 2

Fragmented thoughts on Switzerland

Yong-joo Choi, Vice-President,
aSSIST(Seoul School of Integrated Sciences & Technologies)

Switzerland 1:

The "Lion of the Dead" in Lucerne was designed by Danish sculptor Bertel Thorvaldsen (1770-1844) in 1821 and completed in 1824 by Lukas Ahorn (1789-1856). About 40,000 Swiss mercenaries were killed during the French Revolution in 1789, of which 786 were killed while guarding the Palais des Tuileries on August 10, 1792. At the time when tens of thousands of angry Parisians were marching toward the Tuileries Palace, even the French Army Guards protecting King Louis XVI of France had fled, but none of the Swiss mercenaries were annihilated in the fight against the revolutionary army to protect the king. Although Louis XVI said, "You can withdraw as long as you can," they did not leave until the end. The Lion Monument was erected to commemorate the Swiss mercenaries who died during the French Revolution. The lion symbolizes the dead Swiss mercenaries. The lion protecting the shield engraved with the Bourbon dynasty's lily pattern, which is stabbed through the heart, is a symbol praising the mercenaries' loyalty to the royal family. On the lion statue is the Latin inscription: "HELVETIORUM FIDEI AC VIRTUTI," which means "Loyalty and Bravery of Helvetia (Switzerland)."

Even today, the Vatican only employs Swiss Guards. This speaks to the historical significance of Swiss loyalty. Although it is not their country, Swiss loyalty to whoever has hired them shines throughout its 500-year history. It was this spirit that made Switzerland, a small country with no resources or farmland, the most prosperous country in the world.

Switzerland 2:

Lugano is a beautiful city on the border of Switzerland and Italy. Nearby, in Montagnola, there is a museum by Hermann Hesse. Hermann Hesse liked this place and lived there in the last years of his life. To this day, in Montagnola, Lugano, you can see a tombstone where Hermann Hesse is asleep. Hermann Hesse was born on 2 July 1877 in Germany as the eldest son of his father, Johannes Hesse, a Protestant missionary, and his mother, Marie Gargert. His father was a missionary, so he grew up in a strict environment. It is said that he wandered a lot because he grew up in such a strict and hard home environment, an experience reflected in the novel *Under the Wheel of a Wagon.*

He was very critical of Germany, the homeland that caused World Wars I and II. He eventually abandoned his homeland in anguish and fled to Switzerland, where he lived the rest of his life as a Swiss man. He enjoyed gardening in his later years, and he died on 9 August 1962 in Montagnola. Among his masterpieces are *Damian*, a book that gives readers courage and guidance to live life, and *Siddhartha*, which, like a ray of light, shows the direction of life. These works are famous for expressing the heavy meaning imposed on human existence. These masterpieces prompt readers to ponder the question "How should I live?"

Switzerland 3:

Near Montreux, one of the beautiful towns on the shores of Lake Leman, stands Chillon Castle, which many tourists visit. The castle is said to have been built around the 9th century to collect tolls from merchants crossing the Alps. The Savoy family purchased the castle in the 12th century. The castle is famous for its own sake, but it became even more famous with the publication of renowned British poet Byron's epic "The Prisoner of Chillon."

Francois Bonivard (1496-1570), the abbot of Geneva, who promoted the Reformation in the 16th century, was captured by the Duke of Charles III of Savoy and chained to a pillar in a dungeon in the castle for six years. Bonivard is said to have never renounced his Reformation convictions all throughout his tormented life in the dungeon. Byron was so impressed with the event that it inspired his 392-line epic, and it is said that Byron also had his name engraved on the third pillar of the dungeon. The pillar engraved with Byron's name is an attractive location for countless tourists, where many commemorate their visit by recording video and/or take photos.

What do you think the three Swiss stories have in common?

In the first story, the Swiss mercenaries valued loyalty. They saw loyalty as something that could be exchanged for their very lives.

Regarding the second story, Hermann Hesse spent much of his life contemplating enlightenment. He found his values in the course of his life and acted in such a way to uphold them. The third story tells of how Byron dedicated an epic poem in praise of Bonnie Barr, who did not give in to his bondage and retained his values.

The common core of the three stories is value. The three stories tell about the value of life, value as pursued by an organization, and value as pursued by the world. Companies or products that have sustained performance over a long period of time have a common characteristic; that is, the value a company pursues regarding a product is clear. Companies and products with value are beloved by customers for a long time. If you look at enduring companies and products, they all have value that customers recognize and that anyone can easily accept.

However, maintaining value is not easy. The task is often difficult and painful and sometimes makes one want to give up. The nobler the value, the greater the difficulty of its practice. Therefore, when good values are linked to execution, the results are even more beautiful.

There is external beauty that you can see with your eyes, but there is also internal beauty that you can feel with your heart. In the East and West, the notion of self-sacrifice has spread as a story of salvation and as a symbol of beauty. Values created based on self-sacrifice are considered the most beautiful values. The common denominator of the above stories is self-sacrifice. What was the purpose of the self-sacrifice? It was a sacrifice for value.

The reason the economy develops under a liberal democracy rather than a communist system is simple: Communism is single-dimensionally rigid, but in a liberal democracy, benevolence and strictness co-exist. Outside of types of political systems, there are examples in businesses and families as well. Now, it is becoming a trend of the times to emphasize the social role of companies. The difference between a businessman and a merchant is investment. What will you invest in? Investing in social values is recommended. CSV (creating shared value) and ESG are attracting attention because they focus on businesses' relationships with social values, particularly how companies add social value.

Family peace lies in the husband and wife. The couple is referred to as "one heart." The essence of a successful single-minded body requires freedom not to interfere with each other but simultaneously requires rigor. It should not be too liberal nor should it be too strict. Even after marriage, if you leave a free life to give your partner freedom, your marriage will be in danger. When freedom and rigor are in harmony, mutual trust is created, and a successful marriage is achieved. However, to achieve rigor and freedom, each and every couple needs self-sacrifice, that is, self-sacrifice for the value of family happiness. Therefore, two phrases with opposite meanings, namely "limitless freedom" and "rigor," ironically lead to the common conclusion of trust.

This book is based on the 17 Sustainable Development Goals (SDGs). Professors from the Seoul School of Integrated Science and Technology contributed to this book, selecting the 17 items one by one. The surface tenets of the argument running through the book are topics related to the SDGs, but the inner flow is trust. The practical activities associated with the SDGs were created with the conviction that they would increase trust with respect to each entity.

Each of the 17 SDGs is valid and must be acted upon, but they require self-sacrifice and rigor to put it into practice. However, rigor and self-sacrifice alone are not enough. Systematically, the 17 sublime values should be universalized.

Trust is the ability to fulfill promises. It requires a realistic desire to deliver on promises of outstanding performance. However, aspiration alone is insufficient; there must be a system and an implementation method capable of delivering on the promise.

For a core value to become a special value, become known as a universal value, and permeate into life with common sense, two factors must be present. A successful practice related to values is "education and evaluation." It is for these two reasons that ESG is in the spotlight in the Korean market, but progress toward the SDGs is not booming as much as expected. Various rating systems have been developed in various institutions to evaluate each of the SDGs. On the other hand, education for universalizing SDGs has been lacking.

Fortunately, SDG University was established in Geneva, Switzerland for practical application of the SDGs. The SDG, created in 2015, became an opportunity for worldwide dissemination via education.

I would like to open this book with the hope that SDG University, which is taking its first step, will become the fourth value that symbolizes Switzerland.

Contents

1

Problematics of Using Poverty Data and Poverty Knowledge to Inform Policy Decision Making

Jin-hee Choi

Jin-hee Choi, Ph.D., is an assistant professor at aSSIST(Seoul School of Integrated Sciences & Technologies). She uses a comparative and interdisciplinary approach in her research and teaching. She is interested in investigating diverse sociocultural contexts of adult learning in formal, informal, and non-formal contexts. In particular, she researches how globalization, technology development, and corporatization affect the contemporary learning environment and what adult learning can do to create positive change. She obtained the B.F.A. in Industrial Design at Korea University and M.S. in Cultural Technology at Korea Advanced Institute of Science and Technology (KAIST). She earned her doctorate in Lifelong Learning and Adult Education at the Pennsylvania State University. Currently, she is serving as a board of director at Korean American Academy of Adult and Lifelong Education (KAALE) and an associate editor for Asian Pacific Educational Review (SSCI).

1. Introduction

The purpose of this chapter is to introduce and explore how ending poverty, the first of the 17 Sustainable Development Goals (SDG), has been explored and addressed among engineers and social scientists with respective perspectives. The chapter raises critical questions, such as "What fosters or hinders the eradication of poverty through policy decisions?" Drawing on O'Connor's (2009) problematics of poverty knowledge as a conceptual framework, the current chapter investigates (a) *how* poverty data have been produced through traditional and emerging technologies (e.g., artificial intelligence [AI], big data, and machine learning technology) and (b) *what* drives policy decisions based on poverty data and poverty knowledge. The chapter also explores factors that foster and hinder poverty eradication through an exhaustive literature review. The central argument is that poverty research is a byproduct of the society and the state's public intervention, driven by state ideologies and interests, and is therefore distanced from actually realizing poverty eradication. This chapter is aligned with historical debates on what counts as scientific endeavors with regard to physical, social, cultural, and political forces (Bridgman, 1947; Dushkind, 1953; Michalski, 2022) and the politics of global poverty knowledge (Øyen, 2004; St Clair, 2006), and it calls for critical awareness within the research community and among stakeholders on what counts as and who benefits from poverty knowledge, who should decide, and on what basis the decision should be made.

This chapter consists of three overarching sections, including several sub-sections: (a) an introduction of the advancement of poverty data collection approaches, from traditional household surveys to emerging technologies, aimed at collecting and measuring accurate poverty data and poverty knowledge production; (b) envisioning a mechanism of shaping poverty data into poverty research and how that affects meeting the first goal; and (c) suggestion of changes necessary among scholars, policy makers, and practitioners to achieve policy outcomes to end poverty. In conclusion, the contribution of this chapter is to promote interdisciplinary collaboration among engineering scholars and social scientists, program administrators, policy makers, and advocates to start conversations about developing ways to overcome barriers and obstacles in forging poverty knowledge geared toward poverty eradication, while adequately informed of the knowledge production mechanism in the context of relevant historical debates (Øyen, 2004; St Clair, 2006).

2. Advancement of Data Collection in Scientism: From Surveys to AI, Big Data, and Deep Learning Technologies

Scientists and engineers (Kilic et al., 2017) have emphasized the importance of collecting accurate, low-cost, and systematic data as a means to fight poverty and developing efficient and creative ways to access poverty data using advanced technologies. Traditionally, public data such as household income and consumption were collected, and policy makers applied those data to design and facilitate programs to eradicate poverty. However, the complexity, increasing cost, and sustainability of data collection created problems in acquiring consistent and regular data, particularly in less privileged and marginalized regions and countries. The World Bank reports that it would cost USD 945 million per year to access and track poverty data in less developed regions, particularly those countries that have trouble registering and maintaining data regularity.

Accordingly, for the last three decades, scholars (Alkire, 2007; Tian et al., 2022) have studied methods to collect exhaustive and alternative poverty data through indirect approaches, using existing infrastructure, land use, and mobile/internet usage, instead of traditional survey and public income data. Scholars (Blumenstock et al., 2015; Smith-Clarke et al., 2014) also observed patterns of poverty by viewing private data and internet, mobile phone, and social media usage to infer regional distributions of wealth and poverty. Even in countries where internet business transactions are limited, digital footprints are used to create poverty data.

Recent advances in AI, big data, and machine learning technology have expanded the availability of non-traditional data. Scholars apply high-resolution satellite imagery and nightlight and daylight luminosity data to track economic growth and poverty (Joshua & Blumenstock, 2016; Mwitondi et al., 2020; Zixi, 2021). For instance, night-light satellite images are used to create poverty maps in Latin America and the Caribbean (Andreano et al., 2021). Furthermore, these new technologies allow scholars to revisit traditional surveys and better understand multi-dimensional poverty phenomena (e.g., the probability of a household being poor and poverty rates over time). Machine leaning has been applied to combine datasets in Jordan since 2000 and suggest political, social, and economic changes that affect the poverty that has persisted there over a 20-year period (Alsharkawi et al., 2021).

3. Problematics of Selecting and Transforming Poverty Data into Poverty Knowledge: Political and Ideological Debates and Shifting Policy Decisions

Although scholars apply emerging technologies to access and derive accurate poverty data, social scientists, such as O'Connor (2017), have criticized politics and the ideology of constructing poverty knowledge, that is, the hidden mechanism that shapes knowledge production and knowledge as a product of broader cultural meanings and social situations. Aligned with scholars (Bridgman, 1947; Feynman, 1999) who admit that scientific knowledge cannot be neutral but rather is negotiable, she emphasized the importance of critical awareness of political and ideological orientations that determine research directions.

Having a distinct political and ideological agenda, scholarly discourse on poverty exhibits two distinct research terrains (Chansanam & Li, 2022). Poverty research has been polarized between North American and European scholars with different political and ideological interests. Regarding poverty research under market-oriented neoliberalism, North American scholars emphasize individual responsibility over the social welfare system. Hence, poverty research is deeply interwoven with the politics of class, race, and gender. On the other hand, European scholars pay attention to the welfare responsibility, and policy and practice are geared toward poverty research on the formation and reduction of systematic poverty to improve citizens' living standards.

Scientometric analysis of major publications on poverty between 1964 and 2022 revealed that the dominant discourses diverged between the United States and European countries (e.g., England, the Netherlands, and Sweden) with regard to their particular focus. In the United States, poverty research has been racialized, focusing on the disproportionate sufferings of African Americans in social, financial, and political dimensions. European scholars have suggested issues of rural poverty, risk caused by poverty, and development in poor societies and developing countries. Scholars have criticized the limited effort to conduct scientific investigation and understand poverty in low income, deprived, and under-developed countries. The racialized and disproportionally distributed knowledge production on poverty has created misunderstanding and ignorance regarding the true nature of poverty. Accordingly, O'Connor (2017) emphasized the importance of distinguishing different political meanings attached to poverty knowledge and the interpretation and use of poverty data.

4. Problematic Mechanism of Poverty Knowledge Production

Drawing on O'Connor's (2009) argument of the problematics of poverty knowledge and scientometric analysis of the major publications on poverty between 1964 and 2022 (Chansanam & Li, 2022) as well as recent publications incorporating the use of new technologies (e.g., AI, big data, and machine learning technology), I produced the diagram shown in Figure 1 to illustrate the mechanism of shaping poverty knowledge and the current phenomenon as a consequence of policy decision making.

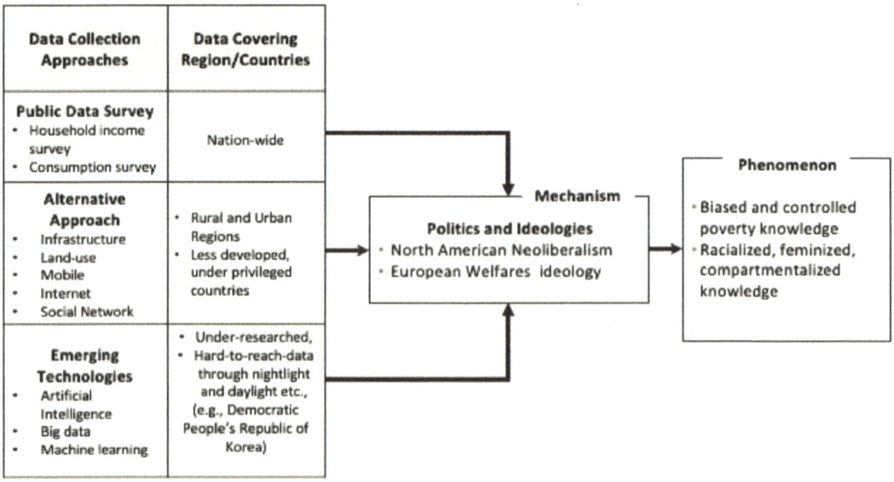

Figure 1. The Development of Poverty Data Collection Approaches, the Poverty Knowledge Production Mechanism (O'Connor, 2009), and the Problematic Phenomenon to Eradicate Poverty

5. Development Implications

- Creating poverty-related knowledge and poverty research costs efforts and resources. Scholars have investigated situations of under-researched regions that suffer from absolute poverty. Scholars, policy makers, and social activists should understand the difference between poverty knowledge and poverty research and seek ways to use scientific knowledge to gain a clear understanding of the poverty issue and the unique situation in rural versus urban areas and across countries.
- Who produces poverty data and poverty knowledge matters to both policy makers and the general public. It is important to map out the politics of interests, who benefits from poverty knowledge, who makes policy decisions (i.e., at the national and transnational levels), and who should participate in it. These are central questions to demystify "the belief in the ignorance of authority" (Feynman, 1999, p. 187). In particular, the explication of those stakeholders and conflicts of interests is critical when engineers start to apply emerging technologies to poverty research because of the amount of data collected and the resulting policy decisions that exert a significant global impact.
- Diversification of research stakeholders is an important issue. The University can contribute to driving and fostering SDG 1 through its opportunities to provide education and research and its potential to invite future stakeholders (e.g., students, faculty, and staff members) to recognize and take necessary social and research

actions (Martínez-Virto & Pérez-Eransus, 2021). Such activities can be linked to the following institutions: Global University Network for Innovation (GUNI), University Social Responsibility Network (USRN), and Talloires Network of Engaged Universities.

- We need to explore the process associated with and consequences of emerging technological development to collect poverty data and produce poverty knowledge and the outcomes of poverty eradication efforts.

6. Conclusion

In this chapter, I explain the advancement of research approaches to collecting data to realize the first SDG goal, which is to end poverty, and critically identify hinderances to achieving the goal. First, I survey the methodological development of poverty data and then highlight the problematics of two overarching mechanisms of poverty knowledge production, drawing on O'Connor's (2017) argument. Further research is needed to explicate the introduction of emerging technologies to poverty data collection and knowledge production.

References

Alkire, S. (2007). The missing dimensions of poverty data: Introduction to the special issue. *Oxford Development Studies, 35*(4), 347-359.

Alsharkawi, A., Al-Fetyani, M., Dawas, M., Saadeh, H., & Alyaman, M. (2021). Poverty classification using machine learning: The case of Jordan. *Sustainability, 13*(3), 1412.

Andreano, M. S., Benedetti, R., Piersimoni, F., & Savio, G. (2021). Mapping poverty of Latin American and Caribbean countries from heaven through night-light satellite images. *Social Indicators Research, 156*(2), 533-562.

Bridgman, P. W. (1947). Scientists and social responsibility. *The Scientific Monthly, 65*(2), 148-154.

Chansanam, W., & Li, C. (2022). Scientometrics of poverty research for sustainability development: Trend analysis of the 1964–2022 data through Scopus. *Sustainability, 14*(9), 5339.

Dushkind, D. (1953). Physical, psychological, cultural and social forces affecting sociological research. *The Journal of Educational Psychology, 27*(2), 80–90.

Feynman, R. P. (1999). *The pleasure of finding things out*. Cambridge, MA: Perseus.

Joshua, B., & Blumenstock, E. (2016). Fighting poverty with data - Machine learning algorithms measure and target poverty. *Journal Science, 353*(6301), 753-754.

Kilic, T., Serajuddin, U., Uematsu, H., & Yoshida, N. (2017). Costing household surveys for monitoring progress toward ending extreme poverty and boosting shared prosperity. *World Bank Policy Research Working Paper,* (7951).

Martínez-Virto, L., & Pérez-Eransus, B. (2021). The role of the public University of Navarre in achieving the 1st SDG for the end of poverty. *Sustainability, 13*(17), 9795.

Michalski, J. H. (2022). The sociological determinants of scientific bias. *Journal of Moral Education, 51*(1), 47-60.

Mwitondi, K. S., Munyakazi, I., & Gatsheni, B. N. (2020). A robust machine learning approach to SDG data segmentation. *Journal of Big Data, 7*(1), 1-17.

O'Connor, A. (2009). *Poverty knowledge: Social science, social policy, and the poor in twentieth-century U.S. history*. Princeton University Press.

Øyen, E. (2004). Poverty production: A different approach to poverty understanding. In *Advances in Sociological Knowledge* (pp. 299-315). VS Verlag für Sozialwissenschaften, Wiesbaden.

St Clair, A. L. (2006). Global poverty: The co-production of knowledge and politics. *Global Social Policy, 6*(1), 57-77.

Tian, F., Wu, B., Zeng, H., Watmough, G. R., Zhang, M., & Li, Y. (2022).

Detecting the linkage between arable land use and poverty using machine learning methods at global perspective. *Geography and Sustainability, 3*(1), 7-20.

Zixi, H. (2021, March). Poverty prediction through machine learning. In *2021 2nd International Conference on E-Commerce and Internet Technology (ECIT)* (pp. 314-324). IEEE.

2

The End of Hunger (ZERO HUNGER)

Young-kee Kim

Mr. Kim had held a number of positions with LG throughout his 36 year's career including LG Electronics' Chief Human Resource Officer (CHO), Head of Corporate Social Responsibility (CSR). After retirng from LG, , Mr. Kim served as the Chairman and CEO of Korea Industrial Safety Association and then as the President and CEO of Korea Elevator Safety Agency, Mr. Kim holds a Ph.D in Union Social Responsibility (USR) from aSSIST(Seoul School of Integrated Sciences & Technologies), Master from Brigham Young University, where he received the Outstanding Global Leader Award, and BA from Sogang University in Seoul. For his dedication to industrial relations in Korea, Mr. Kim received the Korean government's Order of Industrial Service Merit. He has also published a book in English titled Union Social Responsibility for reshaping the roles and responsibilities of labor unions in the future.

1. Introduction

Poverty and hunger are different. Poverty refers to a state in which daily life is hampered by the lack of physical resources that are required to live a minimal human life, whereas hunger refers to a phenomenon that leads to death from a long-lasting lack of food or a serious form of malnutrition. In fact, poverty and hunger are two sides of the same coin; once poverty is resolved, hunger naturally disappears. Nevertheless, hunger is treated as a separate problem because of its gravity.

The Food and Agriculture Organization of the United Nations (FAO) defines starvation as a case in which, for a duration exceeding a year, caloric intake does not meet the minimum required amount of calories to support a sedentary lifestyle. More specifically, starvation is considered a condition in which one cannot consume the minimum amount of calories that an individual needs to live healthy and productively according to gender, age, height, and level of physical activity. This is a similar concept to the chronic hunger mentioned in 'The State of Food Security and Nutrition in the World' jointly prepared by FAO,IFAD, UNICEF, WFP, and WHO.

Hunger is the most serious issue among those addressed by the 17 SDGs. The immediate problem of deaths due to hunger is indeed problematic, but its harm is considered even more serious because malnutrition in infancy directly affects the development of the human body including the brain, thus depriving malnourished children of life opportunities as adults. Moreover, if the problem of hunger is not solved, other sustainable development goals such as education, health, and gender equality will be difficult to achieve.

UN SDG No. 2 presents three interconnected objectives: ending hunger, improving food security and nutrition, and promoting sustainable agriculture. These goals are to be achieved by 2030. However, due to recent issues related to climate change, the novel coronavirus (COVID-19), and prolonged armed conflict, the zero hunger goalpost is gradually moving farther away, as selected in the 2021 Global Hunger Index(GHI), which raised worldwide concern.

SDG No. 2 has eight detailed objectives, from 2.1 to 2.c, which are summarized as follows:

1) The supply of safe and nutritious food to all
2) The end of all forms of malnutrition
3) Increased agricultural productivity and income for small agricultural producers
4) Support for agricultural workers
5) Security of sustainable food production systems and implementation of resilient agricultural practices
6) Maintenance of seed and animal and plant diversity
7) Fair and stable international trade in crops

In this article, we will examine the current status and hunger-related problems around the world and seek solutions.

2. Current status and problems of starvation

As of 2021, the UN reported that 828 million people, nearly 10 percent of the world's population, are starving (World Food Security and Nutrition Status Report, SOFI, 2022). In particular, in the aftermath of the recent pandemic, the hunger population has increased by 150 million, and the hunger crisis is expected to accelerate in 2022 due to the Ukrainian war.

What makes this report even more dismal is that, even considering future economic recovery, 8% of the world's population (670 million) will still face hunger in 2030, making it impossible to achieve the second SDG, which aims to end hunger by 2030.

"The food crisis continues to deteriorate to unprecedented levels, and at the same time, the world situation is becoming more chaotic," said David Beasley, secretary general of the UN World Food Programme (WFP). "The conflict, the climate crisis, and soaring prices along with COVID-19 have brought about the worst-case scenario, such as the perfect storm, and the Ukraine crisis has added to the disaster."

The representative causes of starvation are summarized as the 3Cs: Conflict, Climate Change, and COVID-19. These are followed by systematic poverty and inequality in our society as the next rung of causes of starvation, which are, in turn, followed by unsustainable food systems, lack of investment in agricultural and rural development, insufficient social safety nets and poor governance. A more concerning phenomenon is that several causes of these food crises work in combination simultaneously.

The most critical cause of hunger is conflict. Dominic MacSorley, CEO of Convention Worldwide, which calculates the world's famine index, has argued that "The biggest cause of the food crisis in 2020 was conflict, not COVID-19" and has pointed out that recent conflicts are "localized by more diverse actors, making the impact on hunger more chronic and longer-term." This is because disputes affect the overall food system (production, harvest, transport, supply of inputs, finance, marketing, consumption, etc.).

Underlying the hunger problem is the issue of an unfair food supply chain. Currently, the world's food production exceeds the global population's total food demand. Nevertheless, millions of people are facing starvation, half of whom are farmers or food producers in developing countries. This paradox is due to agricultural policies in developing countries; specifically, because developing countries prioritize the production of preferred crops for markets in developed countries, farmers cannot produce food for themselves or earn sufficient wages to purchase food.

Eric Holt Giménez, Food First Director, argues in his book *Can We Feed the World Without Destroying It?* that most farmers are price recipients, not price determiners for the following reasons. Farmers expend considerable labor planting seeds and wait for months for the grain to be harvested and sold. During that time, farmers cannot move capital. Even if prices fall during the harvest season, farmers cannot slow production to raise prices. It is also not feasible to reduce production to reduce costs. Poor farmers who sell most of their produce immediately after harvest have no options because they need money; they must therefore accept the price determined by the market. Of course, there are farmers who store grains in high-tech facilities and use advanced techniques such as futures trading and linked trading, but these are in the minority, and most are corporate farmers.

According to the World Wide Fund for Nature (WWF), approximately 2.5 billion tons of food are discarded every year worldwide. Following its "global impact of food loss and waste on farms" study, conducted in July 2021, the WWF published the following findings: Farms generate 1.2 billion tons of loss, and retailers and consumers discard 1.3 billion tons every year. This is enough to feed the world's starving people. Losses on farms are mainly caused by unstable food markets and oversupply.

This loss and disposal of food can adversely affect climate change. According to the study, food waste accounts for 10 percent of total greenhouse gas emissions. This is twice the annual emissions of cars operating in the United States and Europe. Despite these detrimental impacts, only 11 of the 192 countries that signed the Paris Climate Agreement included food loss and waste disposal measures in their carbon reduction plans (as of 2021).

Maintaining biodiversity is important for food and agriculture. The average diversity of indigenous species has decreased by 20% (Brondizio et al., 2019). This decline in diversity affects the agricultural ecosystem because it weakens the response to climate change, pests, and pathogens. Strategies that increase productivity by growing only a few crops are not sustainable. Irrigating more land and increasing productivity by adding fertilizers and pesticides are also problematic because these practices affect soil quality in the long run and deplete groundwater.

In the past, it was judged that combining multiple breeding species, chemical fertilizers, powerful pesticides, extensive irrigation, and large agricultural machinery could solve hunger. Holt Giménez has argued that the green revolution already brought about a crisis of overproduction in the 1990s. He believes that increased productivity due to the green revolution resulted in some winners and many losers, which further deepened rural inequality. Furthermore, quite the contrary to solving inequality, GMO, big data, and precision agriculture have aggravated it. In addition to rising inequality in terms of rural income, Holt Giménez believes that the green revolution has resulted in the concentration of land and resources, increased pest problems, and contributed to the loss of agricultural biodiversity, the mass poisoning of farm workers, soil salinity, the depletion and contamination of aquifers, and the erosion of fragile tropical soil.

3. Implications

The problem of starvation is structural and complex. Essentially, two approaches are presented to solve this problem. One is securing food security, and the other is securing food sovereignty.

Food safety is considered secured when everyone has full access to physically and economically sufficient, safe, and nutritious food that is adequate to support a healthy and active life by meeting their dietary needs and food preferences. The four elements that comprise food safety are availability, accessibility, usefulness, and stability. This concept excludes

the way food is grown, the nutritional value of food, food suppliers, and access to food. Therefore, this method alone cannot end hunger.
It is for this reason that the sovereignty of food is emphasized. Here, a 2007 Declaration from La Via Campesina is relevant:

> Food sovereignty is the right to healthy and culturally appropriate food produced through ecologically sound and sustainable means, and [it] places producers, distributors and consumers at the heart of its policy . . . Food sovereignty gives priority to economies and markets based on individual regions and countries and empower[s] production, distribution and consumption of food.

The way we produce and consume determines how our societies are organized. However, the way we organize our society and politics can also determine the way we produce and consume. Holt Giménez has urged us to build an alternative to the capitalist food system in order to feed the world without destroying it. In this sense, securing food sovereignty is a very important issue.

According to the GHI report (2021)

> It is now clearer than ever that the world is hampering the achievement of the Zero Hunger goal by 2030, and that the achievements of the past are built on unsustainable foundations. In order to achieve the Sustainable Development Goals and truly "leave no one behind," we must become more proactive in responding to structural factors such as poverty and inequality that drive people to hunger and malnutrition.

The above-referenced report concludes as follows: "Hunger and malnutrition continue not because there are no solutions, but because of the lack of the political will and resources to put them into practice and to respect, protect and realize the right to food."

From this viewpoint, the philosophy and will of each country's political leaders are important since dispute resolution ultimately requires political solutions and social change. In particular, the cooperation of developed countries is urgently needed. We would benefit from listening to Dr. Vandana Shiva of the Center for Sustainable Food Systems Research, who has stated that cooperation is essential to achieving the mutual goals of zero hunger by 2030 and net zero emissions by 2050.

3

Health and well-being

Jeong-myung Gim

Jeong-myung Gim is Chair Professor of aSSIST(Seoul School of Integrated Sciences & Technologies). He is also Professor Emeritus, Former Dean, and Athletic Director at the College of Arts and Physical Education at Myong Ji University. He is a senior fellow of World Leisure Academy. Professor Gim is an HSE® practitioner certified by Novato Institute and the Director of Korea Somatics Institute. Professor Gim graduated from Seoul National University with BA in Physical Education. He received MA in Sport Management and Ph.D in Sport Philosophy based on Somatic Education at the Ohio State University. He has been Korean Delegate for World Leisure Organization (UN affiliated organization) as a life-member since 1996, working as Board of Directors of WLO during 2006-2011. He was also a Board Member of Korea Independence Hall during 2008-2012. His research interest is Health, Somatic Education, and Leisure Services. He has published several important books in Korean about Health and Somatic Education, such as *Bodyfulness* (2020) and Getting Our Bodies Back (2007) by Christine Caldwell (translator), *The Body of Life*(2013) by Thomas Hanna (translator), Leisure in Your Life by Geoffrey Godbey (co-translator)and *Artful Intelligence: Embodied Rationality*(2016), *America: Manifest Destiny* (2008)and more

Ensure healthy lives and promote well-being for all at all ages

1. Introduction

Well-being is an essential subject when talking about health. Today, health is equalized to not only not having any illness but also leading a happy, satisfactory life. Health is a necessary condition for well-being and well-being is a sufficient condition for health.

According to the eight UN's Millennium Development Goals (MDGs) selected from 2000 to 2015, all of the health-related items are based on reducing the risk of death by combating disease. The main reason for this is that the MDGs were originally created with a focus on developing countries.

In 2015, based on previous analysis of the original, the United Nations expanded to 8MDGS to 17 SDGs(Sustainable Development Goals) from 2016 to 2030, that apply to all countries. The main objective of the MDGs, the eradication of poverty, are handled in the first two goals for the preservation of the global village and humanity in general. The third goal expands upon health as a comprehensive concept of well-being.

The focus of this article is to understand the motives behind the third category (ensuring healthy lives and promoting well-being for all at all ages), and also to suggest a conceptual framework of health and well-being in a larger perspective so as to determine how to improve upon these goals.

2. Problem Statement

The structure of the 17 SDGs announced by the United Nations is generally divided into five categories: people (1-5), growth (8-12), environment (6-7, 13-15), peace (16), and cooperation (17). The third goal, health and well-being, is so central and comprehensive that it is linked not only to other goals in the 'people' category, but also to indicators in other categories.

However, a deeper dive into the subcategories of these goals reveals that they are mostly merely extensions of goals already set in place in the MDGs, such as reducing maternal and infant death rate, managing chronic diseases, and the prevention and interception of infectious diseases. Indicators on life expectancy and Universal Health Coverage(UHC), and studies on subjective well-being were also added. Nevertheless, it is still insufficient to confirm the state of true health and well-being that can control and take responsibility for one's own health only by supplementing these detailed indicators. A sturdy medical system and plentiful medical investments are not all it takes to succeed in the goal for health and well-being, after all.

The UN have tried to make up for this issue by analyzing studies on revealed preferences and satellite accounts, so as to improve the effectiveness of the SDGs. However, these were not investigated as official statistics, and do little in showing sustainability for health and well-being. Therefore, a focus on not only the medical systems of developed countries, but also an encompassing paradigm on active and personal methods to be responsible for one's own health and well-being is needed. To specify, a somatic well-being paradigm that equally applies to all 163 participating nations would create a basis for health and well-being for vastly different cultures.

3. Subject Matter

Somatic well-being, suggested in this study, is a new concept that meets the expanded health concept pursued by the SDGs. Here, 'soma' refers to the living body that an individual experiences inwardly. The body is less of a "patient's" body that could be analyzed, diagnosed, and prescribed by medical doctors from their third point perspective, and more of a subjective body that one can perceive through their own awareness. This body, in right environment or other suitable conditions, can acquire self-healing abilities and responsibility.

Nowadays, for instance, developed countries would be pursuing health and well-being by creating various healing facilities with forests and oceans. In addition, there are many countries that contribute to the health and well-being of their people through traditional therapies, usually involved in integrative mind-body healing. From cutting-edge medical perspective, these methods could encompass fields of study like preventive medicine and integrative mind-body interventions.

From a somatic perspective, a responsible life from a health and well-being aspect would be a life in which a person is self-aware of his/her own body and health, and the freedom of choice to preserve it as such.

Health-conscious somatic activities include daily exercises, yoga practice, meditation, diet planning and other somatic mind-body education. Of course, a medical approach could be also one of those options.

The reason for the third category of the SDGs being health, agreed upon by the global village centered around the UN, is to expand the concept of healthy lives of all mankind into well-being. For most developed countries, since the goals for SDGs #1 and #2 are mostly centered around relief and aid for developing countries, SDGs #3 can realistically be seen as the highest priority on the list.

Economic development and industrial expansion in the 'growth' category may be goals pursued by most countries, but health and well-being goals apply to all countries, whether it be categorized by developed and developing. Of course, the process to achieving well-being is intricately involved with diverse economic systems, and thus may be different for countries with different economy structures. Regardless of the system, however, health and well-being for every person within the community would be a common ultimate goal that all countries strive towards.

The goals of healthy water management, carbon emission reduction, and climate change response that are included in the 'environment' category are also issues of coexistence in the global community that can be hardly solved by a single country. Here, there are cases where the interests of developing countries and developed countries are sharply opposed, but it cannot be understated that the world is already a singular, global community.

As can be inferred from these analyses, goals for well-being may differ in priority from country to country. In most developed countries, the health and well-being of their own people can be the ultimate goal among all other goals, but in some developing countries, this goal is sometimes pushed down by industrial and economic development or capitalist logic, each of whom are more pressing matters for their development.

As such, due to the characteristics of this goal, it is not desirable to put SDGs #3 similar weights by arranging it in parallel with other goals. Even now, the UN are treating SDGs #3 as a special means of connection between the other goals. In fact, for the practical achievement of this goal, it is necessary for all countries to accept this as the ultimate safety valve for human coexistence, as well as for the health and well-being of their citizens.

Therefore, here we propose a new cyclic 'somatic' frame for the SDGs, with SDGs #3 in the center and linked to the other 16 SDGs forming a wheel around it. The original details of the goal such as death rate and life expectancy, while limited, do more than enough to serve as a driving force behind the wheel, from an advanced medical standpoint. The important part is that for health and well-being to be ultimately achieved, we most prioritize the personal, somatic aspect rather than a purely medical one when dealing with the human body.

4. Suggestions

For the proposed wheel with SDGs, it is necessary that SDGs #16 is placed at 12 o'clock position, so that the consensus for human peace would be laid as a premise for the global village. In addition, with #17 (global cooperation) located at the 6 o'clock position, which is the corresponding point, the wheel will attain a driving force.

In the upper right section of the wheel, #1, #2, #4, and #5, focusing on the sustainability of human life are located. In the lower right section, #6, #7, and #13 are placed to maintain the sustainability of the natural ecosystem. #11, #12, #14, and #15 in the upper left are focused on human and nature, while #8, #9, #10 in the upper left are focused on the continuity of each country's growth engine. The latter section is labeled as such because industrial and economic development is still one of the driving forces for health and well-being in the modern world.

Figure 1. Somatic well-being paradigm: restructuring of the SDGs with a focus on health and well-being

5. Conclusion

The formation of SDGs is based on the assessment of MDGs. However, the basis of which they were formed is to set a common goal that humans and nature, and the global village can all be sustained as a cooperative civilization. It is our belief that human health and well-being is not just a singular goal among the 17 SDGs, but an ultimate purpose that the other goals all strive toward. Therefore, the newly proposed wheel-based somatic frame for the SDGs was formed, with health and well-being as the center-force behind its power.

This somatic frame does not linger in prior perception of health, but puts forth a new methodology that applies to all of humanity comprehensively. It will provide an opportunity to realize the goal of somatic health and well-being by promoting the overall improvement of the quality of life.

Somatic health, by definition, is not limited to physical health alone, but encompasses emotional, cognitive, and spiritual well-being as well. It requires a larger perspective than simply analyzing or retrieving physical proof to bettering the quality of life as we feel it. What we feel to be the standards of quality of life or well-being is mainly based on subjective experience. Therefore, we need a somatic frame connected holistically to every dimension of human life beyond the purely medical perspective. Further studies at this point must be conducted on somatic indicators of revealed preferences and their relationships with medical indicators.

4

Culture and Arts Education Connecting the Lives of Active Seniors

Song-hyun Joo

Culture and Arts Education Connecting the Lives of Active Seniors

Song-hyun Joo is an Adjunct Professor at aSSIST(Seoul School of Integrated Sciences & Technologies) in Seoul. She was awarded a PhD from Hanyang University, Seoul, South Korea and holds a BA in n Dance Theory and Aesthetics, and a master in South Korea, both from the University of Ewha Womans University, Seoul, South Korea. She was a director of AI Art Gallery & Associates Art Consulting Company and also worked for Changwon National University (The department of Dance) as an Adjunct Professor. She has been researching, consulting, and teaching in the broad area of art education institutions and global art market. Her research interests include Modern and Contemporary Art and Dance History including AI Art and NFT, Aesthetics, Critical Writing, Global Art Market (Art Collecting, Buying and Selling Art in the Auction market)

1. Korea to Enter a Super-Aging Society

Aging due to a decrease in the birth rate and an increase in average life expectancy is emerging as a global issue. The United Nations (UN) has set the standard age of 65 or older for senior citizens and categorizes a society as "aging" if the proportion of senior citizens in the total population is 7% or higher, "aged" if it is 14% or higher, and "super-aged" if it is 20% or higher.[1] Based on this classification, as of 2013, Japan, Germany, and Italy have already entered an super-aged society, with the elderly population accounting for more than 20% of the total population, and this trend is expected to continue in other countries, with 34 of the world's countries entering an ultra-aged society by 2030.[2]

While many countries are facing aging-related problems, Korea's situation is the most serious in this regard. According to an Organisation for Economic Development and Cooperation (OECD) report, "Korea was the youngest country, but it will change into the oldest country within the next 50 years." Moreover, a UN report predicted that Korea will become an ultra-aged society by 2026.[3] Entering an ultra-aged society only 26 years after becoming an aging society in 2020 is an unprecedented case, with a rate of acceleration that outpaces Japan by a decade.

While super-aging is emerging as the most fundamental problem in our society, a new senior generation of learners has emerged in higher lifelong education. As the number of "active seniors" attempting to develop themselves and strengthen their competencies through lifelong education increases, the traditional negative images of the elderly, such as dependency, incompetency, and weakness, are also gradually improving.

Proposed in 1975 by Bernice Neugarten, a leading aging researcher at the University of Chicago, the term "active senior" is a combination of the words "active," which means "healthy and lively," and "senior," which means "adult."[4] Stating that "Today's elderly are different from yesterday's," Neugarten explained the elderly in detail. He defined the ages of 40 to 49 years as the pre-senior generation, 50 to 75 years as active seniors, and 75 years and older as elderly. He also described persons in the age range of 50 to 75 years as the young-old and those 75 years and older as the old-old. Accordingly, a new group of elderly people aged 50 to 75 years who are fully vital and can actively participate in society based on cultural needs are active seniors. In May 2020, the Ministry of Culture, Sports and Tourism and the National Institute of Korean Language selected *Hwaldongjeok Jangnyeon* as the Korean word to replace active senior.

Unlike past generations, active seniors have a strong desire to live independently and actively, enjoy cultural and leisure life, and contribute to community activities and society through the formation of social networks. This has led to a paradigm shift in the social roles and functions of the senior generation in the social aspect. In terms of lifelong education, various educational methods targeting the senior generation are required, along with the development of faculty's competency, the establishment of an appropriate educational environment, and awareness improvement. Therefore, this paper aims to promote the successful aging of the transitional core generation transitioning from middle- to old age and facilitate stable entry into a super-aging society by suggesting the necessity and revitalization of a plan for cultural arts education that improves the quality of life of the active senior generation.

2. The Necessity of Culture and Arts Education for the Successful Aging of the Active Senior Generation

Recently, interest in old-age life has been increasing rapidly as concerns about entry into an ultra-aging society and views on old-age life have shifted to a long-term viewpoint. Additionally, unlike in the past, as physical and mental health conditions have improved in terms of quality, expectations for old age are growing, and cultural needs are becoming more diversified.

Culture and arts education is based on the same principle that internally integrates culture and art in education beyond the level of simply connecting culture, arts, and education. It refers to understanding the process by which humans shape their own existence through the meaning and inner characteristics of culture and art and understands that this existence becomes reality through culture and art education. In other words, it is based on the philosophical grounding horizon that defines the process of humans becoming themselves in the world and in society and dynamically realizing their own existence as culture. Art contains experiences and forms of culture embedded in such a process and is interpreted in various ways through reproduction. Education functions as a process in which the aforementioned process and the expression of dynamics are present, as opposed to the mere transfer of knowledge. The reality of the culture and arts curriculum is to form humans as cultural beings through the process of achieving this presentation.

The details of culture and arts are applied to strengthen individual creativity, the aesthetic sense, the communication ability, and self-reflection by deriving common goals and meanings from aesthetic, cultural diversity, media, art, leisure, and cultural literacy education. Ultimately, culture and art become reality and content as well as a means to achieve the purpose of education through "culture and arts education."[5]

Doug Herber, director of the Arts Education Program at the National Endowment for the Arts (NEA), explained the effects of arts education with reference to the 4Cs: civilization, communication, creativity, and choice. In other words, it contributes to the improvement of individual welfare by promoting citizenship, improving nonverbal expression, enabling creative communication, fostering creativity, and allowing persons to choose and enjoy their own art among various art forms. The 4Cs imply that the pure function of culture and arts education is to gain understanding and empathy with respect to others by discovering and expressing the essential meaning and value of the human inner self.

3. Examples of Culture and Arts Education for Active Seniors in Korea and Abroad

1) Suwon Lifelong Learning Center's Something School[6]

- Launched in March 2015 as a base camp for active seniors who learn and challenge themselves, the Something School conducts various projects, including educational projects for the elderly. The core of the Something School senior education project is not just offering lectures suitable for the characteristics and orientation of the target age group but creating the will and foundation for members of that group to assert themselves.
- The curriculum is divided into basic, professional, and creative classes. In-depth courses include basic classes such as the Life Class, the Social Economy Academy, the Social Contribution Academy, and the Senior Professional Instructor Training Course and creative classes such as Special Class Woldam, Our Class, and Community.
- The open lecture "Woldam," which began with problem consciousness of young rather than elderly people planning senior activities, involves a monthly talk and "crossing the generation wall." The greatest pride of the Anything School is that seniors plan and execute their own projects.

2) Lifetime Arts[7]

- Lifetime Arts is an educational organization for the elderly based in New Rochelle, New York. Its strategy is to allow the elderly to actively participate in professional and high-quality art programs, and it supports customer-tailored consulting services so that related organizations can design and operate appropriate creative aging programs.
- Representative Lifetime Arts programs include the Lifetime Arts Public Libraries Initiative, community residencies, and the Training Institute Workshop.
- Lifetime Arts offers community residencies to help the elderly enjoy intellectual and creative lives, so that the elderly in New Rochelle can attain a higher level of art education and a deeper understanding of experimental working methods with the help of professional instructors in dance, music, art, literature, and theater.

4. Presenting a New Senior Image of the Active Senior Generation Through Culture and Arts Education

Aging changes the composition of the population due to the effects of extended life expectancy and low birthrates, but such change creates a number of new challenges and possibilities for society as a whole as well as for people's lives. To apply the values and lifestyle options of the 60-year life expectancy era to the 100-year life expectancy era, it is necessary to present a new image of the elderly that acknowledges the change in the existing paradigm, as well as to increase awareness of the ultra-aged society and establish a suitable system. Therefore, this paper focuses on the active senior generation and mentions the need for culture and arts education, since the life characteristics of the transitional generation (aged 50-75 years) transitioning from middle- to old age determine successful aging,[8] which can improve individuals' quality of life before and after that stage. Additionally, the role and value of culture and arts education in promoting self-reflection and an understanding of others in old age are examined through domestic and foreign related cases.

As the number of active seniors increases and the related discourse on culture and arts education becomes more active, relevant academia and institutions should seek organic changes and improvement measures. Participatory measures in this regard include training for professionals, developing educational programs to promote the independence of the senior generation, and establishing an integrated education plan for culture and arts that encompasses all generations.

First, it is necessary to cultivate professionals for the active senior generation. Research and training institutions in culture and arts education centered on the elderly are insufficient in Korea. Academia and the government, including local governments, should pay attention to strengthening the capacity of instructors to develop and apply cultural and artistic theories and practical education plans based on expertise specific to the elderly.

Second, it is necessary to present guidelines for culture and arts education, so that the elderly can practice culture and arts and improve the quality of their daily lives and ultimately develop autonomous elderly-operated clubs. Under the long-term support plan, education programs should be organized as beginner, intermediate, and master classes, and a virtuous cycle should be established, in which learners grow into leaders, and there exists continuous supply and demand.

Third, the scope of culture and arts education for the elderly should be expanded to generation-integrated education and developed into a form of creative education through exchanges with related fields. In the future, creative people will lead innovations that can create high added value and improve living standards. To improve national competitiveness and quality of life in the present era, creative talent is desperately needed. Since culture and arts are widely integrated amongst generations and genres, it is necessary to gradually expand the scope of application to integrated interdisciplinary research, along with generation integration and education programs to foster inter-generational empathy.

Culture and arts education goes beyond simply expanding and disseminating knowledge and experiences based on culture and arts. It is an activity rooted in human existence and related to the basis of individual and community life, and it encompasses the entire process of life itself. Through culture, humans discover their inner self and understand their present, and art is the process of self-fulfillment and the meaningful realization of existence. On this basis, the process of realizing human existence according to its inner principle is the horizon of completely integrated culture and arts education. Culture and art understood on the horizon of semantic behavior centered on the active senior generation will also optimally be oriented according to individual self-understanding and inner belief and further will establish a new elderly figure of the "knowman," which differs completely from the existing negative prejudice.

Through culture and arts education connecting the lives of active seniors, we hope that the message captured in SDG 4—that is, of ensuring inclusive and fair quality education and promoting lifelong learning opportunities for all—will be implemented evenly throughout our society.

Footnote

1 Kim Mi-sook. 〈Socio-economic Problems and Policy Countermeasures in Aging Society: Focusing on the Experience of OECD Countries〉. Korea Institute for Health and Social Affairs , 2003-14 research report. pp 4-7

2 korea Development Institute, 〈aging society,aged society,super-aged society〉 research report https://eiec.kdi.re.kr/material/clickView.do?click_yymm=201512&cidx=2292

3 Statistics Korea, 〈Life table〉, (kostat.go.kr)

4 B. L. Neugarten. 『Middle Age and Aging』, Chicago: University of Chicago Press, 1968. p. 38

5 Seunghwan Shin. 『The Philosophical Foundation of Culture and Arts Education』. Hangil Art Book, 1998. p. 22

6 Suwon Lifelong Learning Center's Something School:I Something School; sourced from: - Daum

7 Lifetime Arts: Lifetime Arts - National Leaders in Creative Aging Program Development

8 Rowe and Khan, renowned in the field of successful aging research in the United States, have argued that a low risk of disease and disability, maintenance of physical and mental functioning, and an active lifestyle are the three keys to successful aging (as in "Health is the key to successful aging"; sourced from: hankookilbo.com).

References

1. B. L. Neugarten. 『Middle Age and Aging』, Chicago: University of Chicago Press, 1968
2. Francis A. McGuire, & Rosangela K. Boyd.『Leisure and Aging』(5th ed.). SAGAMORE Publishing, 2013
3. Silverstein, M., & Parker, M. G, "Leisure activities and quality of life among

the oldest old in Sweden," Research on Aging, 24(5), 2002.

4. Kim Mi-sook. <Socio-economic Problems and Policy Countermeasures in Aging Society: Focusing on the Experience of OECD Countries>. Korea Institute for Health and Social Affairs , 2003-14 research report.
5. Sehoon Kim, Hyungsuk Kim, Manyong Park, Eyoungno Ahn, <Mid- to Long-term Development of Culture and Arts Education>. Korea Culture and Tourism Institute, 2004
6. Seunghwan Shin. 『The Philosophical Foundation of Culture and Arts Education』. Hangil Art Book, 1998
7. korea Development Institute , <aging society,aged society,super-aged society> research report
https://eiec.kdi.re.kr/material/clickView.do?click_yymm=201512&cidx=2292
8. Ministry of Culture, Sports and Tourism : (mcst.go.kr)
9. Suwon Lifelong Learning Center's Something School:l Something Schoo - Daum
10. Statistics Korea, <Life table>, (kostat.go.kr) (kostat.go.kr)
11. 'Lifetime Arts' : Lifetime Arts – National Leaders in Creative Aging Program 11.Development
12. The Korea Times article: Health is the key to successful aging; (hankookilbo.com)

5

Gender equality and women's empowerment: key to achieving business competitiveness

Jae-eun Kim

Jae-eun Kim is the director(professor) of Industry-Academic Cooperation Group at aSSIST(Seoul School of Integrated Sciences & Technologies) in Seoul. She was awarded a PhD from the aSSIST in business administration and a master from Hankuk University of Foreign Studies in Korean-English Translation and Interpretation. She is also serving as a research fellow at IPS (The Institute of Industrial Policy Study). She has been researching, consulting, and teaching in the broad area of corporate social responsibility and sustainability. Her research interests include business administration, business and strategy, corporate social responsibility, sustainability management, CSV(Creating shared value), ESG, compliance and business ethics.

1. Why gender equality is so critical

Gender equality has been one of the core development goals of the international community, even before the adoption of the UN Sustainable Development Goals (SDGs) in 2015. Among the Millennium Development Goals (MDGs), the SDGs' predecessor, "promoting gender equality and strengthening women's empowerment" was listed as the third goal, mainly focusing on bridging gender gap in education. The current SDGs framework reflects the criticism that social discrimination against women and the structural causes of gender discrimination were not addressed properly under the MDG framework, notwithstanding its contribution to girl's education worldwide. This is where the fifth goal, "achieving gender equality and strengthening the capacity of all women and girls" becomes relevant to highlight the importance of gender equality across the sector.

In this context, the term "gender" is important. Why did the UN use "gender" instead of "sex"? Sex is the biological distinction between males and females according to anatomical differences whereas gender refers to the social sex associated with being male or female. In other words, social sex means the role of the male or female. Per the SDGs, equality is to be achieved in women's social roles, and the task of empowering women and girls needs to be approached in an instrumental way.

2. What is the current state of gender equality?

What, then, is the current state of gender equality in Korea? As shown in the table below (detailed goals), assessing gender equality entails examining the degree of gendered disparity in various aspects of society. This paper focuses on women's economic participation and opportunities in society and industry. According to the World Economic Forum's (WEF) 2022 Global Gender Gap Report[1], Korea's gender gap index remained at the bottom of the list, ranking 99th out of the 146 countries surveyed. Korea's score was 0.657 (the closer to 1.0, the higher the gender equality), which is lower than Vietnam's score of 0.705 (ranked 83rd) as well as that of Cambodia (score: 0.690, rank: 98th). Although Korea's ranking rose from 108th at the end of 2019 to 99th in 2022, it remains at the level of underdeveloped countries. Most recently, in the year 2022, the aspects of "economic participation and opportunity" (0.592) and "educational achievement" (0.976) recorded low, ranking 115th and 97th, respectively (additionally, the rankings of health and political power distribution were 52nd and 72nd, respectively). Of a particular note, in terms of opportunities for economic participation, the labor participation rate of Korean women was 53.39%, ranking only 90th in the world, and the wage equality index for men and women performing similar tasks was 0.603, also low at 98th of the countries surveyed.

A survey conducted by the Ministry of Gender Equality and Family showed low equality between male and female median wages. According to the survey of 2,149 listed companies in 2021, the gender wage gap reached 35.9%(average wage per person: 79.8 million won [males]/51.1

million won [females]), which is 2.8 times the average wage gap of 12.8% for companies in OECD countries. Moreover, female executives of listed companies accounted for 5.2%, one-fifth of the average 25.6% of female executives in OECD member countries (the *British Economist*'s the glass ceiling index). Women's employment in retail and tourism has been hit hard by the Covid-19 pandemic, but it is expected that, without a strong policy intervention, it will take a long time for women to secure the same opportunities as men in terms of business, education, and health.

SDG Objectives 5. Detailed Objectives for Ensuring Gender Equality	
5-1.	Eliminate all forms of discrimination against women and girls everywhere.
(…)	
5-5.	Ensure women's full and effective participation and equal opportunity for leadership in all decision-making processes in politics, economics and the public sector.
5-6.	Ensure universal access to sexual and reproductive health and reproductive rights as agreed upon in accordance with the International Conference on Population and Development (ICPD) Action Plan and the Beijing Code of Action and the outcome documents of the Review Conference.
5-7.	Implement reforms in accordance with national law to ensure that women are accorded equal rights to economic resources, as well as equal access to ownership and control over land and other tangible assets, financial services, heritage, and natural resources.
5-8	Strengthen the use of core technologies, especially information and communication technologies, to enhance women's rights and interests.
5-9	Adopt and strengthen robust policies and enforceable legislation to promote gender equality and the rights and interests of women and girls at all levels.

3. How the corporate gender equality mechanism needs to be structured and executed

How, then, should the internal framework for improving gender equality in enterprises be structured and executed? Realizing the value of gender equality can be interpreted in various ways, but the answers will all come down to 'policy and culture' (qualitative performance) and 'numbers' (quantitative performance). Companies usually attempt to adopt policies and strategies that conform not only the related policy and normative environment but also the internal environment; additionally, they measure their quantitative performance and regularly disclose their data to internal and external stakeholders. In this sense, I would like to take a closer look on companies' mechanisms in realizing and promoting gender equality inside the organization based on the SER-M model, which consists with the subject (leaders of the military force), the environment, the resources, and the mechanism, as the factors that determine business results.

Firstly, the drivers that encourage corporate intervention usually originate from the external environment (environment – E). Legislation and standardization of human rights, including gender equality, is in a rapid progress. Among the amendments to the Capital Market Act to be implemented in 2022, it is stipulated that 'a stock-listed corporation with total assets of 2 trillion won or more shall not constitute all directors of the board of directors as directors of a specific gender'. Additionally, the Korea Governance Research Institute (KCGS), one of leading ESG evaluators in Korea, considers the 'number and ratio (%) of female directors' and 'the ratio of female registered executives' in its ESG evaluation of listed companies when evaluating gender diversity on boards of directors. Relevant regulations are being strengthened overseas as well. According to the Directive of the European Parliament and of the Council on improving the gender balance among non-executive directors of companies listed on stock exchanges and related measures[2], at least 40% of outside directors and at least 33% of all directors of listed companies must be of the underrepresented gender.

In line with this trend, BlackRock[3], the world's largest institutional investor, is drafting a policy to oppose the reappointment of directors if there is no female director. In fact, the investor made an opposition to 988 companies in 2021 and 66 in the first quarter of 2022 mainly due to lack of diversity.

Faced with legal challenges, advanced companies are crafting mechanisms to execute strategies in promoting gender equality as a point of differentiation while complying with external requirements: for example, C-level management's commitment (subject), responsive measures to environment (environment), resources to close the gap (resources), gender equality systematic support and promotion and strategy (mechanism), and monitoring and disclosure of key performance (performance), to name a few. Let us examine the mechanisms in more details.

First, corporate management declares its commitment to human rights, including gender equality, both internally and externally as a response to external demands or a differentiating strategy factor (subject – S). The "Subject" factor can be monitored through companies' adoption of ESG or human rights declarations.

Second, enterprises adopt internal and external policies related to gender equality that meet stakeholder requirements. These include not only domestic and foreign laws that affect corporate activities but also regulations and guidelines that have not been enacted but serve as de-facto regulations.

Third, companies allocate their internal resources (resource allocation – R) to achieve gender equality. For example, in the case of existing female employees, policy support can be materialled to maintain a women-friendly working environment while supporting capacity-building. At the same time, they can engage themselves in promoting equality across value chain through applying grading system to transactions with partner companies and suppliers. In addition, their products designed to meet the specific needs of female consumers can be used as medium to promoting gender equality in the market. All these efforts require tangible and intangible resource allocation from within a company.

Fourth, in a bid to impact business performance, companies mediate subject-, environment- and resources-factors to create a unique mechanism. This can be applied to gender equality as well. For example, these mechanisms can include remediation for gender equality, new gender recruitment strategies, human rights impact assessment and development of products and services that minimize human rights risks that all combine to enable gender equality and the empowerment of women.

Fifth, it is possible to measure progress toward realizing gender equality by measuring quantitative and qualitative performance (Performance: P).

For example, indicators can include female employment, policy support for a family-friendly work culture, maternity protection, female leadership, efforts to close the gender wage gap, diversity promotion in top management, and progress toward achieving gender balance in all in-house systems (education, welfare, etc.), to name a few. It is common practices for companies to monitor the status of the company's gender equality on a regular basis.

As seen in the Ser-M model, the detailed goals related to gender equality, especially in business sense, are achieved only when and if gender equality perspectives are integrated across the organization, such as policy, resource allocation, strategy and mechanism, and performance management. In this regard, Korean food company A has explained its efforts to achieve goal #5 through the CEO's declaration of human rights, the introduction of human rights policies reflecting gender equality, gender equality supportive resource allocation, efforts to close wage gap, and monitoring of a ratio of female executives.

Table 1. Analysis of K-ESG guidelines[4] according to the Ser-M-P Model[5] (Focusing on Gender Equality)

Classification	Key Contents	K-ESG Indicators
Subject (S)	CEO/management human rights/ diversity (gender equality) Willingness and formal policy	S-5-1 Human rights policy establishment (human rights declaration, etc.)
Environment (E)	• Legislation and norms related to gender equality • Internal official policies and culture related to gender equality	S-5-1 Establishment of human rights policy
Resource (R)	• Internal policies and resource allocation to support gender equality	

Classification	Key Contents	K-ESG Indicators
Mechanism (M)	• Strategies for utilizing women's human resources	S-2-1 New recruitment and maintenance of employment S-5-2 Human rights risk assessment S-6-1 ESG management of partner companies
Performance (P)	• Achievement of progress toward gender equality • Efforts to spread gender equality outside the company	S-3-1 Percentage of female members S-3-2 Percentage of women's salaries (compared to average salary) G-1-4 Board of directors: gender diversity S-2-2 Percentage of regular workers S-2-3 Voluntary turnover S-2-4 Education and training expenses S-2-5 Benefits

4. The importance of gender equality as a cross-cutting issue

Gender equality goal #5 can have great social impact when and if it is approached as a cross-cutting issue that touches on multiple SDGs, rather than as a single goal. Gender equality is a prerequisite for improving the quality of life in communities and is complementary to other goals such as poverty reduction and food security, climate change mitigation, and a peaceful and inclusive society. For example, goals #8 (decent jobs and economic growth) and #12 (responsible consumption and production) are directly related to the business community's goals for sustainable development. High-quality jobs should not be concentrated on male workforce and gender-balanced perspectives should be incorporated into one's consumption and production strategies. Even if the number of decent jobs is expanded and the goal of high-quality jobs is achieved, failing to achieve gender ratio balance would rather worsen the gender gap, a phenomenon that will hinder the healthy growth of society as a whole. Therefore, the role of companies is even more important in this regard.

5. Conclusion

As reflected in the MDGs, gender inequality is an issue that has persistently hindered the sustainable development of mankind and actions to achieve gender equality can be better emphasized as cross-disciplinary issue that significantly impacts other goals as well. Additionally, in contrast to the MDGs, gender equality as an SDG goal should address the structural causes of gender discrimination in society, including the economy. In particular, from the company's viewpoint, gender equality should be approached as a differentiating factor in corporate management. As pointed out earlier, the reality is that the proportion of women in decision-making positions is not sufficient enough, compared to the proportion of female consumers. As the current decision-making structure has a high risk of failing to have the interests of female consumers reflected in business decisions, companies with a strong policy of diversity is in a better position to improve performance and lower the long-term risk of corporate decision making.

Goldman Sachs, a global investment bank, predicted in a report titled *Womenomics 5.0* in 2019 that 'If the employment rate of women rises to the level of men, Korea's gross domestic product (GDP) will increase by 14.4%.' This means that economic gender equality can contribute to high-quality social growth by expanding women's economic participation and opportunities. In other words, the issue of gender inequality should be approached not merely as a women's problem but rather as a task that would impact the overarching goal of securing the sustainable development and competitiveness of the Korean society.

Footnote

1 The Gender Gap Index (GGI) is a kind of relative evaluation that measures how different women's human rights are from men's rights in a country as an indicator of gender gap, that is, gender differences published annually by the WEF. GGI's evaluation criteria consist of economy (economic participation and opportunity), education (educational achievement), health (health and survival), and politics (political authority)

2 Current regulations and prospects regarding board gender diversity, Shin & Kim LLC, 2022.07.14.

3 BlackRock, Proxy voting Guidelines for Asia ex Japan, Hong Kong, and Chinese securities, Effective as of January 2022; Investment Stewardship Annual Report, 2021; By the numbers-BlackRock Investment Stewardship 1Q 2022 statistics.

4 "K-ESG Guideline: drafted by the Ministry of Trade, Industry and Energy in 2021 to perform as an integrated guidance for local companies and institutions.

5 ser-M framework is designed to analyze one's performance according to mechansim, a dynamic combination of subject factors, environment factors and resources factors (Cho, Dong-sung, 2006)

6

Sustainable Water Use from the Perspective of the National Water Footprint and Virtual Water Trade

Hyo-sook Yim

Hyo-sook Yim is an assistant professor at aSSIST(Seoul School of Integrated Sciences & Technologies). She received a Ph.D. in public administration from Korea University, a master's in system dynamics from the Erasmus Mundus European Master program in System Dynamics, and a master's in environmental planning from Seoul National University. Yim is editor-in-chief of the Korean System Dynamics Review and also serves as a board member of the Korean Society of Environmental Impact Assessment. She conducts interdisciplinary studies on public policies and sustainability science, and she studies systems thinking and system dynamics modeling as her research methodology.

1. Introduction

People tend to consider water is easy to to think of as a renewable resource because it continuously circulates throughout the Earth. However, water is a limited resource. Humans cannot use more water than the amount of freshwater recharged through the water cycle. The amount of water humans can use over a given period has limitations. Therefore, humanity must strive to utilize water sustainably, eliminating water waste and managing water use.

The annual human demand for water use is steadily increasing worldwide. According to the *World Water Development Report 2020*, published by UNESCO, human water use has increased about six-fold over the past 100 years (UNESCO, 2020). If the current trend continues, water scarcity will threaten the survival of humans and ecosystems. Rivers and lakes around the globe are already drying up, and groundwater is being depleted. In addition, some species are endangered by extinction due to contaminated water. Addressing the water scarcity problem requires fair and sustainable water sharing, which is an urgent task for humanity.

Despite the severe water scarcity problem, why are we still not fully aware of the seriousness of water depletion? When people think about the amount of water they use, they only think of the amount of water they consume daily, such as water for drinking, showering, and washing. However, our actual water consumption is much higher because most of the goods and services we consume are produced by using water. For example, the amount of water needed to consume 1 kg of beef is estimated to be 15,400 liters because we feed livestock and need water for beef processing and transportation(Mekonnen & Hoekstra, 2012). It is also known that manufacturing a single tee-shirt consumes 2,700 liters of water.[1] Almost every product and service we consume uses water invisibly. As such, the water consumed for the production process is called 'virtual water', and the total amount of water used in the life cycle of the products and services is called the 'water footprint'.

The water footprint is an indicator designed to quantify the total water usage, including the virtual water. It calculates who uses how much water in an area at any given period. By calculating the water footprint, producers can identify how much water is used at which stage of the supply chain, facilitating efficient water use. In addition, water footprint provides information for consumers to be aware of water usage when choosing products and services. Estimating a country's water footprint can determine the amount of water that people in a country consume. The virtual water trade balance can also confirm the volume of water moving between countries. In this way, water footprint provides information necessary for decision-making so that we can practice effective water use in our daily lives. In particular, it can produce valuable data for confirming the current state of the differences in water use between countries. It can also guide ways for efficient and sustainable water use management measures at the global level.

This chapter examines the status of water use in each country and the flow of water between countries from the perspective of the water footprint and virtual water. Afterward, policy implications for sustainable water use are discussed. Through these contents, we can think about the UN's 6th

Sustainable Development Goal (SDG 6), the common goal of sustainable water use across humanity, which entails healthy and safe water management.

2. National water footprint and virtual water trade

The water footprint is an index of the total amount of freshwater consumed directly and indirectly by a specific user within a certain period (Hoekstra et al., 2011). National water footprint measures the total net amount of water use consumed by residents in a country for a particular year. Thus, it allows the comparison of the water amount consumed by countries. Furthermore, since the water footprint includes virtual water, it is possible to verify the interconnection between geographically distant regions and countries regarding water usage by tracking virtual water flow. The virtual water trade can increase our understanding of the water use gap between nations and the interdependence of water use.

Figure 1 below shows what a national water footprint represents. A country's national water footprint considers both production and consumption. The production side calculates the total water consumed during national production activities. Goods and services produced in one country may be consumed locally or exported to other countries. Since exporting domestic products means transporting virtual water consumed during production to other countries, this part is excluded from the country's water footprint. The consumption aspect of the water footprint calculates all the goods and services consumed by the country's residents.

Import of products from foreign countries means virtual water imports. Therefore, the country's water footprint includes this part. In this way, a country's water footprint calculates the total net amount of water consumed by the people in a nation.

Mekonnen and Hoekstra's (2011) is a representative study in this field, which presents the size of the water footprint of countries worldwide and the current status of the virtual water trade. They calculated the national water footprint from 1996 to 2005, considering all aspects of production and consumption in countries around the world. However, since the results do not reflect the latest data, there is a limitation to grasping the most recent trends.

Other studies focused on calculating the water footprint in a particular country rather than several countries (Da Silva et al., 2016; Konar & Marston, 2020; Schyns, 2013; Steen-Olsen et al., 2012). Some analytical work on countries' water footprint and virtual water trade status has focused on specific industries or items (Caro et al., 2021; Mekonnen & Hoekstra, 2012; Zhai et al., 2019). Since such research only analyzed the current status of water use in specific countries or concerning particular items, it is difficult to comprehensively grasp the current situation of countries' water use based on that body of studies.

Wu et al. (2019) are the most comprehensive and recent of the related studies. They analyzed the water footprint and virtual water trade status of 43 countries using 2014 data. Therefore, in the next section, we examine the current size of the water footprint by country and the status of virtual water trade between countries, focusing on the results reported by Wu et al. (2019).

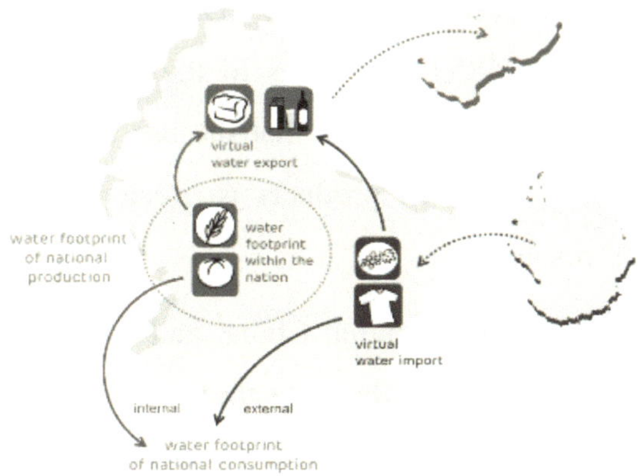

Figure 1. Conceptual diagram of national water footprint calculation
Material: Water footprint network 〈https://waterfootprint.org/〉.

3. Current water footprint and virtual water trade status by country

Figure 2 below shows the result of estimating the water footprint of 43 countries[2] around the world. In the figure, the water footprint is divided into direct freshwater withdrawal (DFW) and virtual water use (VWU). DFW refers to the amount of water the state directly acquires and uses. VWU refers to the water used indirectly through input into product manufacture and service provision. The water footprint results by country show that the world's water use is concentrated in India, China, and the United States.

India has the largest water footprint in the world. India's DFW is 761 Gm^3, and its VWU is 701.7 Gm^3. China ranks second in the world by DFW (607.8 Gm^3) and third by VWU (454 Gm^3). The DFW of the United

States is the third largest in the world (595.7 Gm^3), and its VWU ranks second in the world (485.6 Gm^3). As in the case of the United States, the higher VWU than DFW means that the use of indirect water through the consumption of imported products is greater than the direct use of domestic water resources.

Huge water footprints in India, China, and the United States are also related to their population size because the larger the population, the more water it needs. Considering this, Figure 3 presents the result of dividing countries' virtual water usage by their national population. The result varies significantly across countries, ranging from a minimum of 320 m^3/capita to a maximum of 1,870 m^3/capita. The United States ranks first in the world with 1,870 m^3/capita. The per capita virtual water consumption in the United States is about three times higher than the global average of 545 m^3/capita. Japan (1,181 m^3/capita), the United Kingdom (910 m^3/capita), France (902 m^3/capita), Germany (898 m^3/capita), and South Korea (833 m^3/capita) also have higher consumption than the world average. In contrast, India's per capita virtual water usage remains at the global average (542 m^3/capita), and China's is below the global average (332 m^3/capita). Brazil (409 m^3/capita) also consumes less water than the world average.

Figure 4 shows the scale of virtual water imports and exports by country. The virtual water trade balance in the figure is divided into virtual water intermediate trade balance (VWITB) and virtual water final trade balance (VWFTB). According to the final virtual water trade balance, Japan, the United States, the United Kingdom, Germany, France, and South Korea are water importers, while India, China, Indonesia, and Mexico are water exporters. Water importers depend on foreign water resources for a portion of their water consumption, whereas water exporters use their own water resources to manufacture and export products abroad.

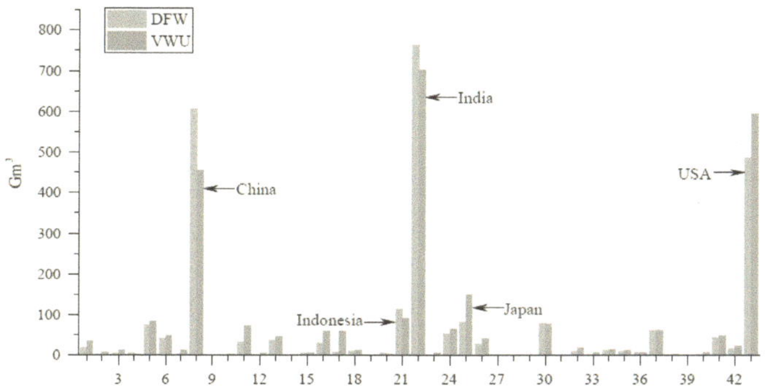

Figure 2. Water footprint by country

Source: Wu et al. (2019, p.798).

Note. Direct freshwater water withdrawal (DFW) refers to direct water usage in the country, and virtual water use (VWU) refers to indirect water usage during production.

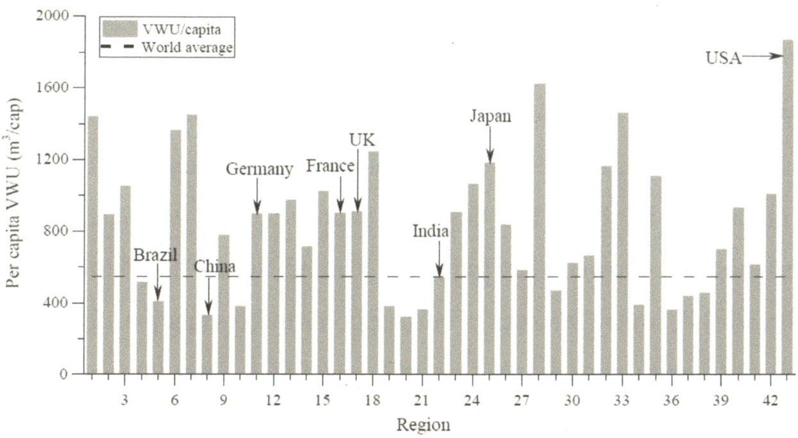

Figure 3. Virtual water usage per person by country

Source: Wu et al. (2019, p. 800).

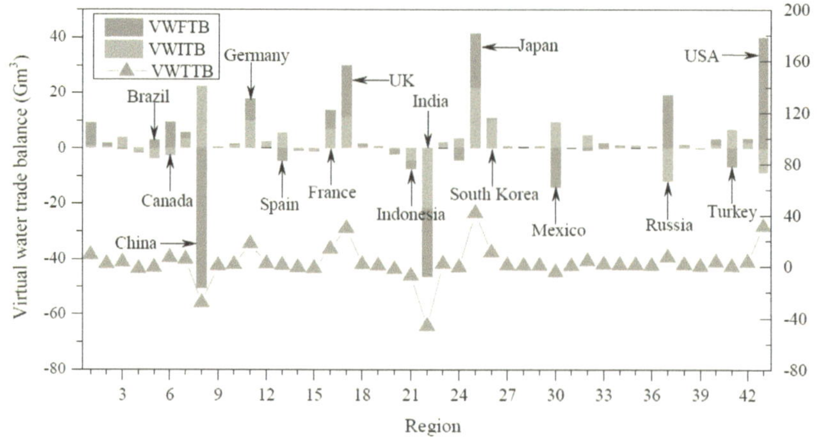

Figure 4. Virtual water trade balance by country

Source: Wu et al. (2019, p.801).

Note. Virtual water final trade balance (VWFTB) refers to the final virtual water trade balance, virtual water intermediate trade balance (VWITB) refers to the total virtual water trade balance, and virtual water total trade balance (VWTTB) refers to the total virtual water trade balance.

4. Future direction for sustainable water use

We examined the size of each country's water footprint (Figure 2) and the status of virtual water use per capita (Figure 3), and we could confirm the imbalance in water use between countries. The estimates of national water footprint showed that India, the United States, and China used most of the world's water resources. Furthermore, the calculation of virtual water usage per capita showed that people in developed countries such as the United States, Japan, the United Kingdom, France, Germany, and South Korea consumed relatively large amounts of water per capita, while people in developing countries such as India, Brazil, and China consumed relatively small amounts of water.

In addition, in the result of the virtual water trade balance (Figure 4), the water usage gap among countries could be confirmed once again. Japan, the United States, the United Kingdom, Germany, France, and South Korea were water importers who relied on foreign sources for some of their water consumption. On the other hand, India, China, Indonesia, and Mexico were classified as water exporters, the countries to meet the demand for overseas water consumption by exporting their water resources.

What we found here is that people in countries with high per capita income use more water than those in countries with low per capita income. This imbalance in the use of water, the world's limited and shared resources, runs counter to the universal principle of human equality. Therefore, efforts will be needed to improve it in the future.

Of course, virtual water trade between countries can help foster efficient use of water from a global perspective. For example, countries with low water reserves can use water cost-effectively by importing virtual water through food and industrial products from water-rich areas. However, an increase in indirect water usage through virtual water trade can lead to a severe problem for sustainable water management.

As indirect water usage increases through virtual water imports, it becomes more challenging to estimate and recognize how much water people actually consume. Also, efforts to save water may not be encouraged in high-income countries, as virtual water imports allow them to consume water at lower prices. Therefore, for a desirable future, policy instruments such as measures to properly reflect the value of the limited resource, water, on the product price would be required to prevent those problems. In other words, from the perspective of sustainable water use, there is a need to focus on developing strategies for internalizing invisible water usage, like virtual water, in everyday consumption and production activities.

5. Concluding remarks

The national water footprint and virtual water trade worldwide allowed us to track the flow of water between spatially and geographically distant countries. It showed that water usage among the world's nations is largely imbalanced. More importantly, it turned out to be a fact that citizens of economically developed countries use significantly more water than those of low-income countries through virtual water trade.

The gap in water usage between people and countries can lead to undesirable consequences regarding sustainable water use. People in countries with high water consumption per capita consume more water through virtual water trade, not direct water intake. This factor likely prevents them from feeling the need for water use management and shields them from paying reasonable costs for water use.

It is necessary to focus more on indirect water, as well as direct water use, to achieve sustainable water use in the future. Along with efforts to overhaul the system so that consumers pay reasonable costs for their water usage, efforts should be made to provide relevant information and enhance education and awareness simultaneously. Furthermore, in the long run, it would be necessary to establish a cooperative system that can promote fair water usage across countries.

Footnote

1 Source: National Geographic. How Your T-Shirt Can Make a Difference. 〈https://video.nationalgeographic.com/video/00000144-0a29-d3cb-a96c-7b2dea6c0000〉.

2 The names of 43 countries by country numbers are 1. Australia, 2. Austria, 3. Belgium, 4. Bulgaria, 5. Brazil, 6. Canada, 7. Switzerland, 8. China, 9. Cyprus, 10. The Czech Republic, 11. Germany, 12. Denmark, 13. Spain, 14. Estonia, 15. Finland, 16. France, 17. England, 18. Greece, 19. Croatia, 20. Hungary, 21. Indonesia, 22. India, 23. Ireland, 24. Italy, 25. Japan, 26. South Korea, 27. Lithuania, 28. Luxembourg, 29. Latvia, 30. Mexico, 31. Malta, 32. Netherlands, 33. Norway, 34. Poland, 35. Portugal, 36. Romania, 37. Russia, 38. Slovakia, 39. Slovenia, 40. Sweden, 41. Turkey, 42. Taiwan, 43. The United States. (Figure 2, Figure 3, and Figure 4 represent countries using the numbers instead of country names.)

7

UN SDG 7: Affordable and Clean Energy

Ho-sang Shin

Ho-sang Shin is currently an Associate Professor and Dean of Academic Affairs at aSSIST(Seoul School of Integrated Sciences & Technologies). He received Bachelor of Engineering degree, Master of Engineering and Doctor of Engineering degrees from Seoul National University. He also received an MBA from a Seoul School of Integrated Sciences and Technologies.

He has been working at a Seoul School of Integrated Sciences and Technologies since 2006 and served as an advisor professor to the president of KOICA from August 2013 to February 2015.

His research fields include system dynamics, complex systems, management simulation, and ODA.

1. UN-SDG 7: Overview of Sustainable Energy

All living things, including humans, maintain life by acquiring energy from their respective life environments. Energy is the most fundamental element of survival, and energy activity is the springboard of economic activity. It is no exaggeration that the difference between developed and under-developed countries is directly related to the difference in the amount of energy available to the individual state.

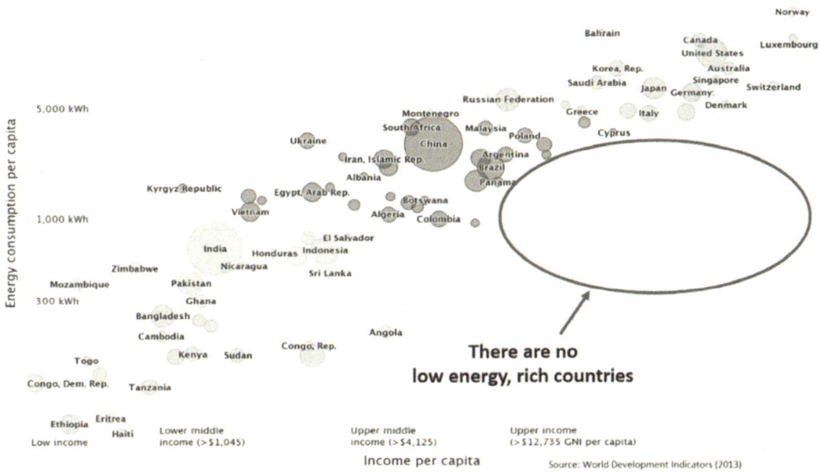

Figure 1. Relationship between income per population and energy consumption per population / World Economic Forum Source: WDI (2013)

1.1 Energy

Energy means the ability to work. Primary energy is directly obtained from nature, and secondary energy is produced in a form that is convenient for utilization, which is achieved by modifying/processing primary energy, such as electricity, city gas, hydrogen, and fuel cells. Renewable energy refers to both new and renewable energy. New energy is based on new physical forces and new materials, and renewable energy is collected from naturally replenished resources. Both types of energy sources are considered future replacements for fossil fuels because the former do not extract energy from stored carbon and have a lesser impact on the climate.[1]

1.2 SDG 7

The UN SDG 7 focus on ensuring "affordable" and "reliable and sustainable modern energy" to ensure the sustainability of human life and the global environment. Access to energy should be "horizontal" to all and "vertical" so that future generations are not left with debt.[2]

UN-SDG 7: Detailed goals

7.1 - Ensure universal access to reliable and modern energy services at reasonable prices by 2030.

7.2 - Significantly increase the proportion of renewable energy in the global energy mix (diversification of energy sources) by 2030.

7.3 - Double the rate of improvement in global energy efficiency by 2030.

7.a - Strengthen international cooperation to promote access to clean energy research and technology development, including renewable energy, energy efficiency, and advanced and cleaner fossil fuel technology, and increase investment in energy infrastructure and clean energy technology by 2030.

7.b - Develop technologies and expand infrastructure to provide modern and sustainable energy services in accordance with national support programs for all in developing countries, especially the poorest, small island developing countries and inland developing countries, by 2030.

SDG 7 presents detailed goals such as providing reliable modern energy at reasonable prices, increasing the proportion of new and renewable energy, doubling the rate of improvement in energy efficiency, promoting investment in energy infrastructure and clean energy technology, and upgrading infrastructure to provide sustainable energy services by 2030.

2. Present conditions

2.1 Domestic status

The Korean Government has presented four detailed goals and seven indicators for eco-friendly production and consumption of energy in the Fourth Basic Plan for Chromogenic Development. The detailed goals are to ensure stable and appropriate access, increase the supply of clean energy from national energy sources, save energy and improve energy efficiency, and minimize air pollution due to energy consumption in the transportation sector.

Table 1 Status of SDG 7 Implementation in Korea

Classification	Detailed items	Current status
7.1 Universal approach to modern energy	7.1.1 Percentage of population with electrical access	100%
	7.1.2 Percentage of population dependent primarily on clean fuel and technology	95%
7.2 Expansion of renewable energy use	7.2.1 Percentage of renewables in final energy consumption	4.3% (2020)

Classification	Detailed items	Current status
7.3 Improve energy efficiency	7.3.1 Energy intensity measured by primary energy and GDP	0.18 TOE/$1,000 (2020)
7.a Promotion of international cooperation and investment related to clean energy	7.a.1 International funding flows to support renewable and clean energy R&D, including hybrid systems in developing countries	
7.b Expansion of infrastructure for energy supply to developing countries	7.b.1 Renewable energy facility capacity in developing countries	305,577 W/person (2019)3

2.2 International status

As of 2014, 85.3% of the world's population could access electricity. This is a 0.3 percentage point increase since 2012. However, 1.06 billion people living mainly in rural areas are still without electricity, half of which reside in sub-Saharan Africa.

As of 2014, access to clean fuel and technology necessary for meal preparation was 57.4%, up slightly from 56.5% in 2012. However, the majority of Asia and sub-Saharan Africa still do not benefit from clean fuel.

The proportion of new and renewable energy in final energy consumption increased slightly from 17.9% in 2012 to 18.3% in 2014. Most of the increase is attributable to renewable energy generated from hydropower and solar and wind power. Despite recent rapid growth in solar and wind power, the ratio of these to total energy consumption remains low. The goal set in SDG 7 is to increase the share of renewable energy in the heat and transport sector, which accounts for 80% of global energy consumption.[3]

3. Discussion and Conclusion

Energy is at the heart of almost all the challenges and opportunities faced in the current global community. Ease of access to energy is essential for all aspects of life, including jobs, security, climate change mitigation, food production, and income growth. Broadly, sustainable energy is an opportunity to fundamentally transform life, the economy, and everything on Earth.[4]

3.1 Sustainable energy

If "sustainability" is interpreted literally, it means that energy is not depleted and is continuously supplied. SDG 7 clarifies its direction as new and renewable energy by referring to modern sustainable energy. Given that renewable energy is expensive compared to traditional energy, it is difficult for poor and developing countries to use renewable energy because its higher energy costs may slow or cause their economic development to fail. Reflecting this situation, the appropriate price is also mentioned. Despite good intentions, "sustainable energy" is a phrase comprising mutually exclusive concepts, especially for developing countries.

Energy, as with all goods, is not uniform in terms of its production and human consumption. It is also regionally unequal, and there are large differences in energy use amongst past/current/future generations. People in developing countries who lack energy-related infrastructure have limited energy access. Another problem is that energy production and use are unequal, and the environmental impact of producing and consuming energy is enormous. Reckless use of fossil fuels has led to greenhouse gas emissions, which is now fueling global climate change.

3.2 Price adequacy, reliability, sustainability, and modernity of energy

At the current level of technological development, a cheap energy supply is difficult to sustain. Energy suppliers' energy production will shrink, and incentives for technological development will disappear. The solution is subsidies or tax benefits, but this route is not feasible for developing countries. Burdening companies may work in the short term, but it is not sustainable. It can be said that energy price aptitude itself contains contradictions. Efforts should be made to convert from energy sources that are expected to be depleted to renewable energy sources, diversify energy sources, and increase energy reserves to ensure the reliability of energy sources. Fossil fuels such as coal, oil, and natural gas are likely to be depleted, and they emit greenhouse gases. Furthermore, nuclear power generation can pose a sustainability problem due to negative environmental effects such as nuclear waste and the consequences of the half-life of radioactive materials. Energy is indispensable for all modern life. Establishing a stable modern energy supply is the most important task for improvement and management per SDG 7.

3.3 Technological development

Energy is technology. Although humanity is making constant efforts to increase the sustainable utilization of energy, it is still insufficient and expensive. Nevertheless, as the sustainability of energy has increased, mankind has graduated to an information society, which has advanced further with the emergence of more ideas and innovative imaginings, such as the generation and transmission of space solar energy beyond renewable energy technology, hydrogen capture in space, low-temperature ammonia hydrogen extraction technology, fusion power generation, electrical energy collection and storage from lightning, solid batteries, thermoelectric devices, and so forth. To achieve the objectives of SDG 7, the development of technologies necessary for the production, movement/storage, and use of energy is paramount.

Footnote

1 https://www.dokdok.co/post/environment-4
2 https://www.unesco.or.kr/data/unesco_news/view/778/1257/page/0?)
3 http://www.hopetofuture.org/bbs/Mboard.asp?Action=view&strBoardID=glec_pds&intSeq=2636
4 https://un-rok.org/ko/%ED%99%9C%EB%8F%99/sdgs-%EC%84%B8%EB%B6%80%EB%82%B4%EC%9A%A9/

References

Korean National Commission for UNESCO (2017), Korean Society and Sustainable Development Goals 7

Korea Energy Economics Institute (2013), Energy Economy

Eun-byul Cho, The Role of Community Energy for Energy Transition: Case study on the apartment community installed household solar photovoltaic panels, Seoul National University Graduate School: Master's thesis in Environmental Planning, 2019

TRACKING SDG7- THE ENERGY PROGRESS REPORT 2022

World Economic Forum, 2013

https://www.dokdok.co/post/environment-4

https://www.unesco.or.kr/data/unesco_news/view/778/1257/page/0?)

https://impactlibrary.net/entry/UN-SDGs-goal-7

http://www.hopetofuture.org/bbs/Mboard.asp?Action=view&strBoardID=glec_pds&intSeq=2636

https://un-rok.org/ko/%ED%99%9C%EB%8F%99/sdgs-%EC%84%B8%EB%B6%80%EB%82%B4%EC%9A%A9/

https://www.yna.co.kr/view/AKR20220408001800082

https://www.hankyung.com/economy/article/202207073709Y

https://trackingsdg7.esmap.org/

8

Promoting Decent Work From the Agape Love Management Perspective

Jong-ouk Park

Jong-ouk Park is the head professor at aSSIST(Seoul School of Integrated Sciences & Technologies) in Seoul Global Lifelong Learning Institute. He graduated from Seoul National University, majoring in agricultural education and rural adult education, and was awarded the M.Div Master of Divinity degree from the Graduate School of Theology at Seoul Theological University.

He received his Ph.D. in Business Administration from aSSIST(Seoul School of Integrated Sciences & Technologies) in Seoul.

His Research fields include Happiness of organizational members, Coaching Leadership, Authentic Leadership, Challenging Stress, Perceived Organizational Support, Resilience, Psychological Empowerment, Grateful Disposition, Job Crafting, Learning Goal Orientation, Feedback Seeking Behavior, Creative Self-Efficacy, Innovative Behavior, Grit , Job Satisfaction, and Growth Mindset.

1. Introduction

The novel coronavirus (COVID-19) pandemic has triggered the worst global economic crisis, the effects of which have led to a setback in the creation of decent work. Although the global economy began to rebound in 2021 as COVID-19 came under reasonable control, concerns about inflation due to rising oil and raw material prices are slowing economic recovery. The conflict in Ukraine is also taking a serious toll on the global economy. This impact is expected to be stronger in the poorest countries than in the developed countries. The tightness of the labor market due to workplace closures in the poorest countries is likely to intensify. In particular, companies in low- and lower middle-income countries are at a disadvantage due to their limited viability. The labor market groups most affected by this global economic crisis are likely to be women, youth, and people with disabilities.

Labor market recovery remains volatile. Many unemployed workers are exposed to informal employment that is far from decent work. Informal jobs have accounted for more than 70% of net job creation in many Latin American countries since mid-2020. Furthermore, increasing poverty and epidemic-related disruptions are causing millions of children to engage in child labor. The number of adolescents without education has increased, and the proportion of females among them is greater. A midst this crisis, it would be very meaningful to reconsider SDG 8. In the face of the global economic crisis, the goal of providing decent work is under great threat. Therefore, it is necessary to clarify the fundamental motives driving efforts to provide decent work.

In this paper, I would like to propose the perspective of agape love as a fundamental motive for creating decent work. Agape love refers to the perspective of feeding and caring in Christian tradition that protects and nurtures the object of love. Agape love means protecting and nurturing the object of love in practice. If there is a concept most similar to agape love, it is parenting, which is when parents raise their children. The agape love perspective is similar to parenting leadership and has the key elements of protection and nurturing. This perspective of agape love can be a key source of motivation for managers to implement the SDGs. Furthermore, the agape love perspective can change the managerial perspective so that the implementation of SDGs can be approached from the perspective of investment, not cost.

2. Raising a question

SDG 8 is related to the economic sector and reads as follows: "Promote sustained, inclusive and sustainable economic growth, full and productive employment and decent work for all." SDG 8 has mainly been discussed in terms of concepts connected with international development cooperation based on economic perspectives. However, in this paper, I would like to discuss such job creation from the perspective of corporate management. Furthermore, I would like to discuss managers' motivation to create decent work primarily from the perspective of agape love, which is based on love for current organizational members and those who will become future organizational members, as well as broader agape love for all of humanity.

Discussing SDG 8 from the economic viewpoint and from the viewpoint of international development cooperation is a positive starting point, but it is difficult to see that these activities are effective in terms of sustainability. For SDG 8 to be truly sustainable, the management viewpoint within companies that create jobs should be reviewed. If continuous job creation is possible for businesses, the potential gains from such job creation could exceed that of national aid. Therefore, this paper discusses job creation from a management perspective, rather than taking an international development cooperative approach from an economic perspective.

Furthermore, job creation is an investment, not a cost, and the motivation for this investment is similar to parents' intensive investment for a certain period of time in love with their children. When job creation is continued for the poorest countries with the Agape love motive, such investment can be strategically correct decision-making for the sustainable management of companies. From the perspective of Agape Love Management, I would like to discuss SDG 8's goal of creating decent work. Managers may view creating and providing decent work in the least developed countries or developing countries as a huge cost. However, if we approach this from the agape love management perspective of protecting children, adolescents, and women who are in desperate need of decent work and nurturing them so that they become independent and can partner with global companies, then this is an investment, not an expense. If the practice of approaching the SDGs from the perspective of agape love characterized by protection and nurturing is adopted, I am certain that mankind will enter a more co-prosperous stage.

3. Global companies' SDG 8 practice

1) A case study on LG Chem's sustainable supply chain management

Cobalt, a major raw material used in the production of lithium-ion batteries, is one of the scarcest minerals. The Democratic Republic of the Congo produces 60% of the world's cobalt and is known for exploiting child labor and poor working conditions. Children are often sent to collect cobalt because of the narrow tunnels in the mines. There have been cases where mines collapsed, and children lost their lives. Under these circumstances, LG Chem is trying to solve the children's human rights issue in the context of cobalt mining in Congo. LG Chem ensures that the raw materials it receives do not include cobalt mined through child labor. To this end, in 2018, they did their due diligence with regard to small-scale mines in Congo to ascertain whether child labor was being used and disclosed the results on their website. In 2022, LG Chem upgraded to the Responsible Business Alliance (RBA), which is the upper level of RMI. LG Chem is building a management system within the value chain by applying the standards of international organizations such as the UN and the OECD, as well as the RBA standards.

LG Chem's efforts to implement SDG 8 are in line with the company's commitment to "management with respect for humanity," and this management philosophy of LG Chem's is in line with the agape love perspective. In particular, LG Chem's efforts to eradicate child labor in small-scale mines in the Democratic Republic of Congo are aimed at protecting children involved in cobalt mining. LG Chem is implementing a pre-emptive policy to protect children from exploitation and mine collapse accidents in connection with cobalt mining labor. Such child labor has been eradicated by creating an environment where they cannot come to poor labor sites. Recognizing that one company's power is not enough, LG Chem is collaborating with global organizations to foster an environment where child labor can be fully eradicated and the decency of the jobs connected with cobalt mining can be enhanced. LG Chem's practice can be seen as a very positive case in terms of the exercise of protective and nurturing agape love.

2) Nestle's solution to increase farm income to address child labor risks

On January 28, 2022, Nestlé announced a new plan to address child labor risks in cocoa production. The plan includes an innovative income promotion program aimed at improving the livelihoods of cocoa farmers. Cash incentives paid directly to cocoa farmers are disbursed for specific activities such as enrolling children in school and pruning. Nestlé's new initiative also supports the company's efforts to transform the global sourcing of cocoa to achieve full traceability and segregation of cocoa products. Nestlé plans to invest about 1.7 trillion won by 2030, more than three times the current annual investment. Nestlé will present a range of products using sustainably sourced cocoa in this innovative program, and this product lineup will provide consumers with the opportunity to help improve families' livelihoods and protect children.

Nestlé's case can be seen as a more advanced model from the viewpoint of agape love. Nestlé did not stop at eradicating child labor in cocoa production or protecting children from indecent work. Nestlé has created an ecosystem where children can receive an education. Nestlé offers preferential incentives to female farmers in families who send their children to school. Furthermore, a system was established to provide additional benefits by continuously monitoring children's attendance at school. Nestlé has therefore enabled children to be nurtured in the right direction through regular education.

This strategic plan of Nestlé's can be seen as a very desirable model that has elements of agape love in the sense of protection and nurture. Furthermore, it is expected that farmers who achieve self-reliance through these incentives will be able to invest more in their children's education. In turn, children who are educated in this way will have the opportunity to grow to adulthood and generate more income. Nestlé's case is a representative example of achieving SDG 8 from the perspective of agape love, with its two key elements of protection and nurture. Through this investment, Nestlé is expected to secure a stable and traceable supply of cocoa. Therefore, Nestlé's case can be seen as more sustainable.

3) A Case Study on Samsung Electronics' Job Creation in Korea

According to the Samsung Electronics Sustainable Management Report 2022, recent activities related to SDG 8 are summarized as follows. First, the company participates in nurturing startups to secure social-level innovation and new growth engines. Second, investment in R&D and productivity improvement in small and medium-sized enterprises (SMEs) is expanding. Samsung Electronics is operating C-Lab to contribute to the vitalization of the domestic startup ecosystem. Furthermore, C-Lab Spin-off is a system that supports spin-off start-ups by selecting excellent projects with high external growth potential from among the tasks nurtured through C-Lab Inside, an in-house venture program. Through C-Lab Outside, the company has fostered a cumulative 400 competitive startups from 2015 to the present.

Representative examples of smart factory support are as follows. Ace Life is a bidet company located in Asan, Chungcheongnam-do. Demand for bidets surged due to the COVID-19 outbreak, resulting in a surge in orders. At that time, Ace Life's production capacity was around 20,000 units per month. To meet the monthly order volume of 32,000 units, it was necessary to improve the supply capacity. As a result of receiving various forms of support from Samsung Electronics, the company's production capacity increased by 110% (42,000 units per month). Management performance is also expected to increase annual sales by KRW 7.5 billion, and 16 additional people were hired. Consequently, the case of Samsung Electronics has contributed to the creation of decent jobs in Korea.

These various efforts comprising the case of Samsung Electronics are judged to contribute greatly to the creation of decent jobs in Korea. The smart factory support initiative implemented as part of support for SMEs actually effectively fosters SMEs and contributes not only to the improvement of sales but also to job creation. Samsung Electronics has not only protected poor SMEs but has also contributed to the growth of SMEs and the creation of decent jobs by nurturing their technological prowess. The case of Samsung Electronics can be seen as having the core elements of the agape love perspective, namely protection and nurture. From the perspective of agape love, SMEs are protected and nurtured to create decent jobs.

Furthermore, C-Lab Inside and Outside are avenues through which Samsung Electronics nurtures startups by creating an ecosystem where startups can launch their own businesses with various technologies, laying the foundation for creating decent jobs in the future. In particular, through future technological development projects, it has contributed to the improvement of technological skills that can be the basis for start-ups. In this way, Samsung Electronics has contributed to increasing the number of decent jobs by improving technology and encouraging start-ups based on application of these technologies. Samsung Electronics' efforts to realize SDG 8 can be viewed as a representative example of the agape love perspective of establishing a protective and nurturing ecosystem for the creation of decent jobs.

4. Concluding Remarks

This paper examines SDG 8, the creation of decent work, from the perspective of agape love, that is, protecting and nurturing the object of love. The efforts of LG Chem, Nestlé, and Samsung Electronics, which are global companies at home and abroad, to achieve SDG 8 can be seen as representative examples of agape love. These global companies' efforts are not reduced to simple cost; rather, they are investments on which there will be returns to the benefit of the investor companies. From this viewpoint, it is judged that the most ideal case is that of Nestlé. The case of Samsung Electronics is also a very good example, but it is thought that the company is replacing the policy that the government should do, not the company. In the case of LG Chem, while the protection the company offers is strong, nurturing is weak.

In contrast, in Nestle's case, the more incentive policies are implemented, the more stable and traceable the supply of cocoa, which brings benefits from the company's investment. The Nestlé example could be a truly sustainable one. Therefore, to achieve SDG 8 and create true sustainability and decent work, both key elements of the agape love perspective, namely protection and nurturing, should be included, as in the case of Nestlé. Concepts such as simple corporate social responsibility have limitations in terms of sustainability. By comparison, the agape love management model, in which elements of protection and nurturing are applied simultaneously, is expected to have more sustainability. Therefore, the process of creating decent work in companies in the future should develop in a direction that has both elements of the agape love perspective: protection and nurturing.

The agape love perspective may appear to be a concept far removed from management. Ultimately, however, it would not be an exaggeration to say that mankind has developed by virtue of the agape love perspective, that is, the practice of parenting leadership acting to protect and nurture. Today, mankind is highly developed, yet humanity has not been able to solve the problem of economic inequality. Therefore, the UN's SDGs are considered to be the practice of macro-parental leadership to solve the problem of human inequality and develop into better mankind through the noble human-to-human goal of protecting and nurturing. Achieving this noble goal will require motivation from the agape love perspective.

If we look at the SDGs through the lens of protecting and nurturing humanity toward the realization of a more mature humanity, the human race will take a step forward. From this viewpoint, companies' implementation of the SDGs will be a noble step. In particular, if one of a company's unique purposes is to create jobs, companies' efforts to achieve SDG 8 are even more sublime. Furthermore, it is clear that companies' efforts to create decent work are not just costs, but investments toward the future and humanity. To drive this paradigm shift, the perspective of agape love characterized by protection and nurturing is presented. Based on this, we recommend the development of agape love management.

9

Sustainable Development Goal 9 – Industry, Innovation, and Infrastructure

Kyung-geun Lee

Sustainable Development Goal 9 Industry, Innovation and Infrastructure

Kyung-geun Lee is a professor at aSSIST(Seoul School of Integrated Sciences & Technologies). He was awarded a PhD from Sciences-Po University in Paris, France (i.e., Foundation Nationale des Sciences Politiques). He holds a BA in Business Administration from Seoul National University in South Korea and a MBA from University of California at Berkeley in the US. He has been the leader of the tax counseling part of Yulchon LLC since 2007, recognized by Chambers Asia-Pacific as a leading professional in Band 1 Group of Tax Consultants. He used to work in Korea's Ministry of Economy and Finance as high level official and served the OECD as a member of the Secretariat during 1999 ~2002.

1. Preface

The ninth of the 17 Sustainable Development Goals (SDGs) adopted by the UN General Assembly in 2015, SDG 9, is concerned with “industry, innovation and infrastructure” and aims to create the foundation for sustainable industrialization through the establishment of infrastructure necessary to support society as well as innovation and development. This concept can be easily understood by perusing Korea Telecom(“KT”)’s GIGA ISLAND project, which is described below.

Internet access used to be difficult on Maheshkhali Island in Bangladesh due to poor IT infrastructure, but thanks to KT’s network construction and support, users can now use the Internet at a speed of up to 100 Mbps. Consequently, young students have been able to receive video-based education, and islanders have been able to generate higher profits through e-commerce. Prior to the introduction of e-commerce, agricultural product distribution entailed paying high commissions to middlemen due to physical restrictions, but with the advent of e-commerce, the intermediate margin disappeared, allowing residents to earn over three times more than before. Moreover, on the Maheshkhali island, where medical infrastructure was lacking, KT has provided mobile ultrasound and blood analyzers, allowing doctors to remotely and regularly diagnose residents[1]. As such, when IT and related infrastructure are established in a specific community, development follows in various fields such as education, economic activity, and medical care. This is what SDG 9 aims to achieve.

2. Detailed targets and indicators of SDG 9

2.1 UN SDG 9

SDG 9, an industry-sector SDG, consists of five specific targets and three implementation targets, with 12 indicators. The specific targets are related to infrastructure, industrialization, financial services, eco-friendly processes, and strengthening R&D, respectively, and the implementation targets can be divided into 'the expanding support for infrastructure construction in developing countries', 'the support for R&D and innovation in developing countries', and 'the support for access to ICT in the least developed countries'. Details are given in Table 1 below.[2]

Table 1. Specific Targets and Indicators of UN-SDG 9

	Specific Targets of UN-SDG 9	Metric indicators
Infrastructure	9.1 Develop quality, reliable, sustainable and resilient infrastructure, including regional and trans-border infrastructure, to support economic development and human well-being, with a focus on affordable and fare access for all	9.1.1 Proportion of the rural population who live within 2 km of all-season road 9.1.2 Passengers and freight volumes, by mode of transport
Industrialization	9.2 Promote inclusive and sustainable industrialization, and by 2030, to raise significantly the industry's share of employment and the GDP in line with national circumstances as well as to double its share in least developed countries	9.2.1 Manufacturing value added as a proportion of GDP and per capita 9.2.2 Manufacturing employment as a proportion of total employment

	Specific Targets of UN-SDG 9	Metric indicators
	9.3 Increase the access of small-scale industrial and other enterprises, particularly in developing countries, to finance services including affordable credit and their integration into value chains and markets	9.3.1 Proportion of small-scale industries in total industrial value-added 9.3.2 Proportion of small-scale industries with a loan or line of credit
	9.4 By 2030, upgrade infrastructure and retrofit industries to make them sustainable, with increased resource-use efficiency and greater adoption of clean and environmentally sound technologies and industrial processes, with all countries taking action in accordance with their respective capabilities	9.4.1 CO_2 emissions per unit of value added
Innovation	9.5 Enhance scientific research, upgrade the technological capabilities of industrial sectors in all countries, in particular developing countries, including, by 2030, encouraging innovation and substantially increasing the number of research and development workers per 1 million people and public and private research and development spending	9.5.1 Research and development expenditure as a proportion of GDP 9.5.2 Number of Researchers (in full-time equivalent) per million inhabitants
Fulfillment goals	9.a Facilitate sustainable and resilient infrastructure development in developing countries through enhanced financial, technological and technical support to African countries, least developed countries, landlocked developing countries and Small Island Developing States	9.a.1 Total official international support (official development assistance plus other official flows) to infrastructure

	Specific Targets of UN-SDG 9	Metric indicators
	9.b Support domestic technological development, research and innovation in developing countries, including by ensuring a conducive policy environment for, inter alia, industrial diversification and value addition to commodities	9.b.1 Proportion of medium and high-tech industry value added in total value added
	9.c Significantly increase access to information and communication technology and strive to provide universal and affordable access to the Internet in least developed countries by 2020	9.c.1 The number of mobile cellphone subscriptions (per 100 people), and the share of a given population using the internet (on any device)

2.2 Targets and Indicators for Establishing SDG 9 in Korea (K-SDG 9)

The Korean government set the strengthening of sustainable development as a national task in 2018 and established the Korean Sustainability Development Goals (K-SDGs) at the end of 2018.[3] The targets and indicators for the K-SDGs were established by collecting opinions from the entire nation and using the UN-SDGs as a benchmark, albeit to the exclusion of specific targets and indicators not suited for Korea[4] and with the addition of indicators absent from the UN-SDGs that have been deemed relevant to the Korean situation.[5]

Against this background, the goals and indicators[6] of SDG 9 following the establishment of the K-SDGs were determined as follows.

Table 2. K-SDG 9 Specific Targets and Indicators Established in 2018

Target	Number	Specific Targets	Indicators(Unit)
Building infra-structure, expansion of R&D, and economic growth	9-1	Making efforts to provide welfare services and information access to the majority of the public in a stable manner	Proportion of Road penetration (km/1,000 people)
			Weight of transportation consumption per household
			Accessibility of the to digital information among vulnerable social group (%)
	9-2	Securing industrial competitiveness by pursuing industrial diversity and laying the foundation for sustainable corporate activities	Proportion of small-scale industries with a loan and the line of credit
	9-3	Strengthening international competitiveness by building technological capabilities and promoting advanced technology commercialization	Success rate of commercialization of R&D projects (%)
	9-4	Contributing to national economic growth through the expansion of national research personnel and capital and the planning and execution of appropriate research	R&D expenditure relative to GDP
	9-5	Pursuing industrialization with high resource efficiency through environmentally friendly industrial activities and technological innovation	CO2 emissions per unit of value-added
			Domestic resource productivity (GDP/DMC),[7] Resource strength (DMC/GDP)

3. Raising a question

In the period 2001-2015, before the UN promoted its SDGs, the UN promoted projects focused on social development in developing countries under the Millennium Development Goals (MDGs). Unlike the MDGs, the SDGs set global goals beyond the social development of developing countries and encompassing fields such as economics, society, and the environment. Accordingly, advanced countries are not only required to support the achievement of the goals of developing countries as in the past but must also play an active role in realizing sustainable development in their own countries.[8]

The UN has also presented guidelines for voluntary national assessment (VNR),[9] along with (i) creating a sense of ownership of SDGs,[10] (ii) building SDGs into the domestic system,[11] (iii) integrating the three aspects of the SDGs, the economy, and the social environment,[12] (iv) applying the inclusiveness principle,[13] (v) and developing institutional mechanisms.[14]

Further, regarding the establishment of digital infrastructure, which is closely related to SDG 9, the importance of inclusiveness principle has been emphasized. Regarding digital transformation, which countries around the world have recently pursued, the UNDP[15] expressed its position that "Digital transformation is an important driver for achieving SDGs, but digital transformation itself does not automatically guarantee the achievement of SDGs." It also pointed out that "2.9 billion people are still offline, and 96% of them live in developing countries." In this context, "To build a more open, transparent and sustainable society, digital transformation must be intentionally inclusive, and digital transformation must be carefully designed and implemented with people and human rights at the center of all aspects. In sum, the UNDP has emphasized that while digital transformation is not an end in itself, it is an enabler for more significant social change at scale.[16] The UNDP's position seems to shed light on the direction of setting goals and establishing policies related to K-SDG 9 in the future.

4. A Case Study of Ukraine's Digital Transformation Initiative[17]

In 2019, the Ukrainian government established the Ministry of Digital Transformation to lead the government's digital transformation project. Within 5 months of its launch, the Digital Transformation Department launched a mobile app called Diia to provide more than a dozen public e-services. However, the Ministry of Digital Transformation found that half of Ukraine's population did not use Diia's e-services until autumn 2020.

The UNDP helped overcome this challenge by commissioning a study which showed that eServices did not fully comply with international accessibility standards such as the Web Content Accessibility Guidelines, thus limiting accessibility. By taking a "rights-based approach" to user design - through documenting the user journey of people with a disability, it demonstrated the value of rethinking the eService design.

As a result, the Ministry has decided to review the eService websites. As part of the process, UNDP organized a training event on how to make websites and other digital resources inclusive, which was attended by more than 200 civil servants and government officials from across Ukraine.

As of April 2022, Diia's users exceeded 17 million, nearly a third of the Ukrainian population, as a result of the Ukrainian government's efforts. After the outbreak of war in Ukraine in February 2022, the Ukrainian government began providing necessary public e-services amidst war via Diia. For example, developing and operationalizing a system to register property damaged by war can allow the government to offer proper compensation in the future. Additionally, existing platforms and processes are being used to implement necessary digital public services amidst war, such as submission of evidence of internally displaced people or unemployment through Diia.

The inclusive design of the service platform and the intentional attempt to increase accessibility helped its people during times of crisis.

5. Performance and limitations of digital infrastructure in Korea

As shown in Table 2 above, Korea selected the indicator "digital information accessibility (%) of the vulnerable class" as an indicator of the detailed target set at 9-1 at the time of the establishment of the K-SDGs. However, as shown in Table 1, this indicator is not included in the

UN-SDGs' measurement index and is an index that the Korean government developed by itself. This shows that even before the UNDP explicitly presented its guidelines, the Korean government, in the process of constructing digital infrastructure, considered it important to ensure that no segments of its population are alienated from digital information (i.e., inclusiveness principle). In 2021, the government partially revised the existing targets and indicators of the K-SDGs when establishing the 4th Sustainable Development Basic Plan, especially the existing indicators for digital information on K-SDG 9-1. The original indicator was "accessibility of digital information (%) among the vulnerable group," but in 2021, it was changed to "level of digital information (%) received by the vulnerable group compared to the general public" because, while Korea's "digital information accessibility (%) among the vulnerable group" in 2019 was 91.7%, the levels of digital informatization (69.9%), information capacity (60.2%), and utilization (68.8%) of the vulnerable group vis-à-vis the general republic were still low[18]

Most of the SDG measurement indicators related to industrialization in Korea are already quite advanced by international standards. Manufacturing value-added ratio to GDP, manufacturing employment ratio, R&D expenditure ratio to GDP, R&D researcher count ratio, and infrastructure ODA ratio are superior, compared not only with the international community as a whole but also with even developed countries.

To evaluate the degree of implementation of SDGs in each country, the UN advisory body, the Sustainable Development Solutions Network (SDSN), calculates each country's SDG index and dashboard annually and publishes the results in a report.[19] The degree of implementation of the SDGs in the industrial sector is evaluated according to 11 indicators for the industrial, innovation, and infrastructure sectors. The 2018 report supplemented the analysis by adding two new indicators to the existing set. The existing indicators used to evaluate the degree of implementation of SDG 9 are Internet population, mobile broadband subscription, infrastructure as a whole, logistics, universities, science and technology journals, R&D, and patents. According to these indicators, Korea has been evaluated as continuously maintaining its status, after having already achieved its goals.

In the 2018 evaluation of Korea, focusing on these indicators, it seems that inclusiveness and the achievement of overall national goals were taken into account in evaluating the implementation status, as evidenced by the addition of indicators of the Internet accessibility gap by income and the proportion of women in science and engineering. However, regarding the indicator newly added in 2018, the degree of achievement of Korea's goal was evaluated to be low. In other words, in 2017, Korea's goal achievement was evaluated as good according to all indicators and as positive in terms of achieving SDG 9 overall, but in 2018, it was evaluated as 13.0% according to the Internet accessibility gap by income and 24% according to the ratio of women in science and technology, which negatively affected the overall evaluation.[20]

According to the Sustainable Development Report (2022), an evaluation report that the SDSN issued in 2022, the Internet accessibility gap by income has significantly improved, up to 0.8%, which is evaluated as in the green. However, the proportion of women in the science and engineering sector still has room to be improved, although there has been a slight increase in the proportion, up to 25.2%.

Taken together, it can be seen that the inclusiveness of the digital field in Korea has improved significantly in recent years. Additionally, in the case of Korea, it can be self-evaluated that goal achievement in fields related to SDG 9 is extremely high, except for the insufficient entry of women into the science and technology field.

However, the meaning of this positive evaluation is somewhat tarnished considering that the ODA level index (% of GNI), which is an indicator of SDG 17, showing Korea's ODA level, was only 0.2 according to the 2022 report and has consequently been evaluated as in the red. In other words, digital inclusion is very high in Korea, but internationally, the ODA scale is very low, so the degree to which Korea contributes to achieving SDG 9 in the international community must have been evaluated as low.[21] It can therefore be said that by international standards, inclusion in the digital field is low.

6. Conclusion

Compared to other OECD countries, Korea has done much to strengthen SDG 9. As such, this is an area in which Korea has a comparative advantage over other countries in terms of related technologies and promotion policies. Recently, the UNDP emphasized that inclusion should be secured as early as the design stage to promote SDG 9, especially digital transformation. Reflection on Korea's recent experience shows that

Korea has achieved its goal quickly in terms of domestic inclusion. However, considering that the absolute value of Korea's ODA level is low, inclusion per SDG 9 by international standards is still considered to be quite low.

Considering the fact that it has been growing with foreign aid for a considerable period of time since the point in time when it was among the poorest countries, Korea, which has already entered the ranks of advanced countries, should now pay its debts to the international community in earnest. Moreover, considering that Korea's soft power has increased due to the recent Korean Wave, Korea's international influence has also increased, and it is believed that developing countries' demand for Korean aid has increased as well.

Therefore, if Korea drastically increases the absolute size of its ODA and focuses on building digital infrastructure that can bring advantages, in the future, it will contribute greatly to achieving not only K-SDGs but also UN-SDGs, the goal set up for the whole world.

Footnote

1 https://m.blog.naver.com/ewklcamp11/221971888271 (Access date: July 30, 2022)

2 SY Lim, IC Kim, and SI Jeong, Law Research on Climate Change and Sustainable Development: Understanding and Promoting the Domestic Implementation of the Locally Sustainable Development Goals (SDGs) in the Industry-Industrial Sector, Korea Legislative Research Institute, 2018, pp. 28-29.

3 Sustainable Development Committee of Ministry of Environment, *Report on the Korea's Establishment of Sustainable Development Goals*, July 2019.7., p6.

4 For example, indicators such as female genital mutilation, eradication of outdoor defecation, cross-border water resource management, eradication of child labor, and guarantee of access to vaccines were excluded, as they were judged inappropriate for the domestic situation based on opinions canvassed among stakeholders and the public.

5 For example, indicators such as preparedness for chronic diseases, overcoming the low birth rate, integrated water quality management, development of alternative plastic materials, and establishment of a permanent peace system between the two Koreas were added.

6 Sustainable Development Committee of Ministry of Environment, *ibid*, p46.

7 Domestic material consumption

8 Accordingly, the UN recommends that not only developing countries but also developed countries conduct a voluntary national review to monitor and announce the degree of implementation of the SDGs.

9 Voluntary National Review is part of the SDGs follow-up and review mechanism. The UN requires that each Member State voluntarily review regular and comprehensive progress and present the results at the High-Level Forum for Sustainable Development (HLPF). Korea participated in VNR in 2016.

10 To facilitate the implementation of the SDGs, it is necessary to raise awareness of the SDGs among various stakeholders, including the central government, local governments, and legislative bodies, and to increase these stakeholders' sense of ownership through dissemination of governmental information on the SDGs.

11 Governments should identify the major challenges and difficulties they face in implementing the SDGs, integrate the SDGs and targets into the domestic framework in accordance with national circumstances, and promote policy coherence and interconnection. For example, the SDGs should be integrated into the national vision, the national development plan, and the sustainable development strategy to facilitate domestic implementation.

12 Since the SDGs are closely related, it is necessary to understand the interrelationships amongst the various goals and conduct activities to foster coordination and cooperation among relevant sectors and institutions. Integrating the economic, social, and environmental aspects of the SDGs means making efforts such as institutional coordination for integrated policy making. The government should try to identify the major obstacles to integrating the three aspects of the SDGs and generate effective solutions.

13 In line with the SDGs' common principle of leaving no one behind, governments should take steps to address inequality. In particular, it is necessary to identify the vulnerable groups in the country and make efforts to address the causes of their vulnerability. To this end, the underprivileged can be embraced through the preparation and implementation of policies that reduce inequality and eliminate discrimination.

14 The government should develop a stronger and more inclusive institutional mechanism by examining and improving institutional means for the implementation of the SDGs. To achieve the SDGs, various organizations from all sectors must participate and harmonize, so cooperation between various ministries and sectors is required.

15 United Nations Development Programme

16 United Nations Development Programme – Chief Digital Office, *Inclusive by Design: Accelerating Digital Transformation for the Global Goals*, 2022, p. 4.

17 UNDP, *ibid.*, pp. 26–27.

18 Joint Task Force of the Relevant Ministries, *The 4th Basic Plan for Sustainable Development 2021–2940 – Part 2*, 2021, p. 155..

19 The SDG Index and Dashboards report had been published annually since 2016, and the report title was revised to "Sustainable Development Report" in 2019.

20 SDSN & Bertelsmanss Stifung, *SDX Index and Dashboards Report 2018 – Global Responsibilities*, 2018, p. 259.

21 SDSN & Bertelsmanss Stifung, *Sustainable Development Report 2022*, 2022., p. 265.

10

Inequality

Tae-yeon Oh

Tae-yeon Oh is an assistant professor at aSSIST(Seoul School of Integrated Sciences & Technologies) in Seoul. He was awarded a PhD from Seoul National University, Seoul, South Korea, and holds a master of arts in economics and bachelor of science in mathematics, both from the Sogang University, Seoul, South Korea. He was an assistant professor of sports analytics at the University of Mississippi, MS, USA, and post-doctoral research fellow at the Center for Global Sports and Recreation Studies at the Hong Kong Baptist University, Hong Kong SAR. He has been researching, consulting, and teaching in the broad area of sports media management, sports media communication, sports analytics, esports management and AI & big data analytics. His research interests include consumer behavior including fans, users, gamers and sports participants in digital platforms.

1. Introduction

To discuss inequality, one must clearly define the term. Jean-Jacques Rousseau published the book *The Theory of Human Inequality* (*Discours sur l'origine et lés bonds de l'inégalité parmiles hommes*) in 1755, in which Rousseau expresses the belief that inequality began when humans started to own private property. In other words, humans in their natural state are good beings, but in the social state, they are evil. Subsequently, in *Emile* and *The Social Contract*, Rousseau predicted that citizens could enjoy equality before the law and social freedom. Here, it is worth noting that inequality exists in the distribution of goods and in disparate social statuses. Notably, the issue of inequality regarding social status was abolished in most countries as liberal ideas spread and civil revolutions occurred, and the majority of countries have established, at least legally, a society in which all citizens enjoy equal rights. However, economic inequality, or the unequal distribution of goods, still exists, and the imbalance in this regard is worsening (Chancel et al., 2022).

Among the 17 sustainable development goals (SDGs) the UN has proposed, inequality encompasses various phenomena, but through analysis of policy directions, wealth inequality between countries has been identified as a major concern (UN, 2022). From this viewpoint, this article attempts to examine the problem of economic inequality between countries, at which the UN is aiming, and explore future directions for alleviating it.

2. Raising a question

The issue of inequality that the UN is trying to solve is ultimately a problem of the income gap between countries. The income gap itself is a natural phenomenon, and if you try to forcibly solve it, it can have a reverse effect. For example, many researchers have emphasized that the income gap and inequality act as the driving force for economic rise to the ranks of the upper class. Additionally, considering the fall of communist countries, which were huge socials experiments, it is evident that solving the problem of inequality through equal distribution of goods is not of great practical benefit.

However, recently, inequality has been causing problems in various fields beyond the bias toward wealth, the most representative of which is the refugee problem. People become refugees for various reasons, but refugeeism largely occurs because the state does not guarantee the lives of citizens, essentially because the country is not sufficiently wealthy to take responsibility for citizens in an emergency. Large-scale migrants constitute a similar example. Many citizens of underdeveloped countries move to developed countries through various methods because their expected income in their homeland differs significantly from that in migrant countries. These migrants are often encounter discrimination in their destination countries, and regardless of their abilities, they mainly engage in low-wage labor to support the societal infrastructure. This inequality problem is not just a matter of a difference in the quality of life; it entails exposure to risks in many fields such as health and the environment.

Compounding the aforementioned, there exists the problem that the current changes in the social structure are deepening inequality between countries. As evidenced by the current global supply chain, the roles of low-wage countries in charge of production, resource-rich countries in charge of resource supply and demand, and advanced countries in charge of technological development and product development are segregated. Therefore, in the case of low-wage countries, it is inevitable to adopt an industrial structure centered on simple labor, which contributes to the widening technology gap with advanced countries (Costinot et al., 2012). Amidst the fourth industrial revolution and the acceleration of digital transformation, advanced countries with sufficient technological development infrastructure are recording strong economic growth, while middle and underdeveloped countries are seeing slow growth (Dong-young, 2022). Additionally, with the agreement on environmental protection, developed countries are already shifting toward low-pollution carbon-neutral industry, but in middle-income countries, development is still insufficient to support the shift to low-pollution industry. In this situation, seeking carbon neutrality will eventually be an act of clearing the ladder for underdeveloped or developing countries. Many researchers have predicted that the Great Divergence, which appeared between developed and developing countries during the Industrial Revolution in the 18th century, will reappear (Young-chang, 2017). Unfortunately, two world wars and the intervening Great Depression were the biggest factors that eased the Great Quarter of the 18th century.

The WID has confirmed through a report observation of signs that, especially given the trajectory of the novel coronavirus (COVID-19) pandemic over the past few years, the gap between countries has widened. Therefore, I would like to examine the UN's current attempts to resolve inequality and explore possible supplementation.

3. Present relevant phenomena and exemplar cases

The UN has proposed ten targets and indicators to resolve inequality (UN, 2022). The first of these is to significantly improve income levels in low-income countries. The second and third goals are to eliminate gender, race, and other discrimination, and the fourth and seventh are to regulate countries by introducing progressive policies on income, finance, distribution, etc. To achieve this, the last three targets are the formation of a consultative body with the WTO, the establishment of a transnational regulatory system, and finally, the reduction of remittance fees for migrant workers. Most of these goals will depend on the ability of the UN's leadership to break down the global capitalist structure and implement financial reforms. However, the goals subsequent to the fourth one are difficult to achieve in reality considering the shape/composition of the current UN leadership. In that case, should we just watch as the fourth industrial revolution and extreme polarization of the carbon economy and the post-pandemic economy unfold?

If the project to overcome the current status of inequality is structured from the perspective of SER-M (Cho, 2015), it can be analyzed as follows. Firstly, the UN is the subject of the project (S). The UN is a loose coalition amongst countries, and in this context, it is impossible to establish active policies through strong leadership. The UN is a consultative body comprising numerous countries, but it is also an organization that vests great power in five permanent members. The project environment (E) has problems such as the global supply chain, the fourth industrial revolution, and carbon neutrality. Finally, resources (R) can be seen as countries' manpower, capital, and technology. Combining these three factors results in six possible permutations. Among them, it can be seen that the UN's action goals are creative mechanism strategies such as SER or SRE. In particular, projects related to global regulation and wealth distribution can be seen as reflecting a typical environmental creation mechanism strategy (SER). However, as Cho (2015) noted, the creative mechanism centered on this subject is a strategy that requires strong leadership to guide the organization according to the specified vision. Therefore, it is a mechanism that is difficult to apply under the current UN system. An appropriate mechanism according to the nature of the project would be the environmental innovation mechanism (RSE) or the resource innovation mechanism (ESR). Considering that the flow of external environmental changes is irreversible, the current inequality problem can be solved through the ESR.

With the ESR mechanism, the subject adapts to the environment and establishes a project strategy in the direction of innovating available resources. Regarding the problem of inequality, resources (R) are very disproportionately distributed amongst countries. Capital and technology are concentrated in a small number of developed countries, most of which face the problem of a decreased working population due to low birthrates and aging populations. In particular, the low-skilled low-wage working population continues to decline. However, in low-income countries, capital and technology are relatively insufficient to provide sufficient jobs for the workforce. The fourth industrial revolution and environmental problems, which are environmental factors, are making it increasingly difficult for underdeveloped countries to succeed through the fast follower strategy. Even in developed countries, the phenomenon of job concentration is worsening, and manpower shortage is emerging. Therefore, it is necessary to establish a strategy that will allow the subject (S), that is, the UN, to innovate resources to adapt to the environment and resolve inequality. Therefore, I would like to present an international large-scale labor migration strategy.

4. Directions or implications for development

According to studies such as Weyl (2016) and Clemens (2011), the migration of workers from low- to high-income countries is known to be a corridor in which rich countries can move into low-income countries without imposing economic losses on citizens of developed countries. Of course, reckless migration of workers can cause various social problems such as social division, religious conflict, and security issues. In the case of European countries with a long history of migrant workers, those countries have already experienced various concomitant social problems (Hui-won & Sung-chul, 2010). In particular, residential discrimination, security issues, and expansion of political influence due to an increase in the number of settled people are emerging as serious social problems. However, effective wealth transfer can be achieved by establishing standards for education and the treatment of migrant workers through international cooperation and introducing laws that limit political influence (voting rights, permanent residency, etc.) while allowing long-term stay. Developed countries such as the United States and Europe, as well as many emerging countries in East Asia, including the Republic of Korea, are currently responding to the decreased labor demand by accepting a large number of migrant workers (Kim, 1994). However, the current migrant labor method is based on personal job search activities or agreements between countries. In other words, there are no unified conditions to address problems such as the working environment, educational opportunities, and the quality of life of migrant workers. Therefore, if the UN establishes a transnational consultative body to manage and distribute migrant workers, much of the current migrant worker problems can be solved. Additionally, if migrant workers are provided with continuous educational opportunities in the process of migration as well as post-migration, the problem of educational inequality can be ameliorated. In this process, if the wealth of advanced countries is transferred to low-income countries through migrant workers and an environment is created where highly educated personnel can return to their respective home countries and pass on various technical and industrial know-how in the long run, it will show a positive signal in terms of solving inequality.

5. Conclusion

Based on the SER-M model, this study attempted to examine whether the UN's current strategy to combat inequality is valid and suggest alternatives. The UN's goal is obviously a long-term project, and it is an innovative way to resolve income inequality between countries. The problem is that the leadership of the UN, the subject of the project, is unsuitable for strategically adopting the necessary mechanism. Therefore, I have proposed an alternative that entails approaching the problem of inequality through a resource innovation mechanism as a short- to -medium-term strategy. In particular, it will be possible to form a consultative body to bridge countries and transfer the wealth of developed countries to developing countries through the migration of workers, thus playing an additional role in resolving educational inequality in this process.

Furthermore, if these transnational consultative bodies are successfully established, UN leadership will gain more authority, and this will serve as a foundation for long-term progress toward the SER mechanism the UN plans to strategically apply.

References

Chancel, L., Piketty, T., Saez, E., & Zucman, G. (2022). *World inequality report 2022*. World Inequality Lab.

Clemens, M. A. (2011). Economics and emigration: Trillion-dollar bills on the sidewalk? *Journal of Economic Perspectives*, *25*(3), 83-106.

Costinot, A., Vogel, J., & Wang, S. (2012). Global supply chains and wage inequality. *American Economic Review*, *102*(3), 396-401.

United Nations. (2022). *The sustainable development goals report*.

United Nations. (2022). *Reduce inequality within and among countries*. https://sdgs.un.org/goals/goal10

Glen Weyl, E. (2018). The openness–equality trade-off in global redistribution. *The Economic Journal*, *128*(612), F1-F36.

Kang, H.W. & Kang, S. C. (2010) Change in Immigration Policy and Governance for Social Integration in Germany. Journal of Korean Association for Policy Sciences

Kim, D. Y. (2020. 5. 25) Concerns about income inequality caused by technological development. Hankook Ilbo.

Kim, J. S, (1994) Countermeasures for Foreign Workers. Health and Social Welfare Review

Lee, Y. C. (2017.2.21) The 4th industrial revolution may increase polarization and inequality. Hankook Ilbo

Cho, D. S. (2015). Mechanism-based perspective: a new paradigm for integrated management. Seoul: Seoul Business and Economics

11

City Development Strategy with SDGs

Joong-ho Chang

Joong-ho Chang is an associate professor at aSSIST(Seoul School of Integrated Sciences and Technologies) in Seoul. He was awarded a PhD and MS degree from Texas A&M University US, majoring in Computer Engineering. He graduated Yonsei University in Seoul, majoring in Electronic Engineering. Before he joined to aSSIST, he was the senior vice president of Homeplus, which is a large retail company in Korea, also Emart and GS homeshopping. He also has worked in business strategy consulting firms, such as PwC and Deloit. His research interests include AI strategy and Big data analysis and platform, Digital Marketing, and business model development.

1. Introduction

Of the 17 United Nations Sustainable Development Goals (UN-SDGs), the most common and necessary item of concern in developed and developing countries is SDG 11, the goal of creating resilient and sustainable cities and residences. Among the SDGs, the goals related to cities are presented in various ways and divided into ten detailed items. Presently, population growth in cities is exploding, as the industrial base in rural areas weakens worldwide. In developing countries, poor people flock to cities because of their low economic standards, which causes numerous problems because governments cannot develop cities or install infrastructure. However, this is not a concern for developed countries. The UN has proposed and manages specific indicators to solve these urban problems and establish and achieve practical goals; these apply not only to national governments but also to responsible companies, social organizations, and schools, which must establish and continuously conduct their respective R&R. The British Forestry Commission has suggested economy, environment, and society as three factors for the sustainable development of cities (Figure 1). Ultimately, the problem with respect to the city is economical, that is, related to money and the various environments comprising the city's basic infrastructure, particularly the elements of transportation, the communication infrastructure environment, and the garbage and air environment, which are especially important. A single entity cannot handle all of these components, and governments, corporations, organizations, schools, and citizens must all contribute to forming society and continue to provide education and guidance to drive a change in consciousness. In this article, I would like to examine three methods of solving urgent urban problems, based on the three elements of sustainable development.

2. Raising a question

Of the ten goals pertaining to creating resilient and sustainable cities and residences, the three most closely affecting ordinary citizens in both developed and developing countries are housing, transportation, and urban waste. Gradually, the various types of city infrastructure, especially human housing, have become insufficient, and due to the rise in housing prices, young and elderly people with weak economic returns are being pushed into impoverished spaces. Additionally, in large cities that lack proper transportation infrastructure, many problems occur due to limited roads to accommodate individuals' use of cars and motorcycles. In particular, places such as Jakarta, Indonesia and Ho Chi Minh City, Vietnam have seen very large industrial losses due to heavy traffic jams caused by cars and motorcycles at a time when public transportation comprising buses and subway trains is poor. Finally, the disparity regarding people's living standards, hygiene, and living environment is very large in cities where infrastructure or systems such as waste separation or disposal have been inadequately developed. In particular, the explosive increase in household waste due to population growth has already exceeded the limit that any city can handle. In this article, I would like to examine in detail development strategies, examples, and implications related to the three key items mentioned above among the goals toward realizing resilient and sustainable cities and identify alternative resolutions.

3. Present relevant phenomena and exemplar cases

The first issue, residential space, is more serious in developed countries. Of course, the severity is not comparable to the poorest countries, but the recent global urban problem has caused housing prices to soar, for many reasons, and the number of dwellings needed on limited land is increasing. Urban redevelopment requires higher levels of housing, but it entails many legal and economic procedures and costs. As a solution to the housing problem, the concept of ownership has recently changed to the concept of use, and there is a movement to maximize the efficiency of space by sharing. Unlike young people, the elderly do not have to maintain their homes for an extended period of time, and there is a trend of pursuing community life, encompassing aspects such as meals, hobbies, and health care, by moving into retirement towns and nursing facilities. Through related classes and people's practice of community living, housing problems, loneliness, and cost efficiency can be solved.

The second problem, transportation infrastructure, requires enormous amounts of money at the national SOC level, and the best practices with regard to urban transportation issues can be seen in Seoul, South Korea. Seoul and Gyeonggi are overcrowded, with 25 million people, which is more than 50% of the nation's population, but infrastructural systems such as buses and subway trains are well established, and transportation payment and scheduling information are integrated through IOT services. Advanced transportation infrastructure such as Seoul's is uncommon, even in large cities in advanced countries such as the United States and European countries. Achieving this degree of sophistication has been possible for Seoul by virtue of a digital powerhouse where public government agencies integrate and settle payment and operation information for each operator, such as subway trains, wide-area buses, branch buses, and village buses, so that citizens can use the system very cheaply and conveniently via a single card. Developing countries such as Indonesia and Vietnam, which lack transportation infrastructure in cities, can eliminate the stigma of being a "transportation hell" and reduce the cost of public and personal transportation by planning to build the most basic of subway and wide-area bus lines.

Third is the issue of urban waste overflow. As the population of a city increases, the amount of garbage naturally increases, with a tremendous increase in the amount of chemical waste in particular, such as plastic and vinyl, especially due to the explosive increase in non-face-to-face online shopping including food delivery with the onset of the novel coronavirus (COVID-19) pandemic. Citizens of developing as well as developed countries do not have proper food and beverage waste disposal facilities, and developing country residents use disposable products more than those of developed countries because of the former's unsuitable households; hence, the level of environmental waste is alarmingly high. Fortunately, with recent technological developments, waste plastic and vinyl can be chemically treated and reprocessed using various petroleum derivatives to produce recycled plastics, vinyl, and chemical fibers. The development of industries that selectively collect, treat, and provide waste to reprocessing companies or factories is therefore important. Additionally, citizens should be encouraged to refrain from using or limit their use of disposable or plastic products. To achieve this, it is necessary to increase their level of consciousness. Further, even if some persons are uncomfortable, they should be encouraged to participate in separate waste collection, which will elevate the overall cultural level of the citizenry.

The above three major SDG-related issues reflect trends and examples of solution directions relevant to realizing resilient and sustainable cities.

4. Directions and implications for development

The trends and solutions mentioned pertain to the three main items presented in Chapter 3. The most important aspect of implementing this plan is raising citizens' consciousness. Housing, transportation, and environmental issues are too vast to be solved through infrastructural investment alone. In line with the three elements for the sustainable development of cities according to the British Forestry Commission, heightened awareness is necessary in urban communities regarding the economy, the environment, and the society. If the perspective of individual housing ownership changes to the concept of sharing, allowing landlords to offer shared leisure spaces and spreading the culture of shared housing spaces among youth, many residential problems can be solved. Regarding the problem of transportation, citizens will benefit from infrastructure built through bold governmental investments when the perception of the culture of using individual motorcycles or cars changes in favor of public transportation. Regarding the use of big data platforms, in the era of these platforms' development, the use of transportation data collected through smartphones, including with respect to shared cars and taxis, is a way to reduce traffic in the city center, even minimally. Most citizens of even developing countries have mobile phones, and companies are emerging to solve traffic problems by creating transportation data and sharing economies. Environmental problems such as garbage are among the most important areas for change regarding the perspective of citizens and society. No matter how high-tech the waste disposal facilities, they will be useless if waste is not properly classified, collected, and disposed. Additionally, the cultural movement to refrain from using disposable products as much as possible is also a means of solving some fundamental problems. To this end, cultural movements related to various subjects and communities within the overarching concept of society are essential.

5. Concluding remarks

The UN has defined 17 SDGs and set goals for creating resilient and sustainable cities and residences. Among these is the promotion of cultural movements to raise awareness, increase empathy, and encourage concrete practice and sustainability with respect to governments, businesses, social groups, and communities around the world. Problems such as housing, transportation, and garbage cannot be solved unless people's perceptions and behaviors undergo direct change. Digital transformation elements such as digital information sharing, activating practical communities through mobile platforms, big residential data, establishing transportation infrastructure and information and payment systems, operationalizing various incentives and penalty provisions for garbage separation, and developing technology for monitoring and controlling local communities can play a major role. Recently, many cities, not only in Korea but also abroad, have undertaken smart city projects intended to solve fundamental problems and change citizens' perceptions through the digital transformation of cities. The development of sustainable cities is not only a matter of national tasks and homework but also a matter of civic consciousness, and therein lies the solution.

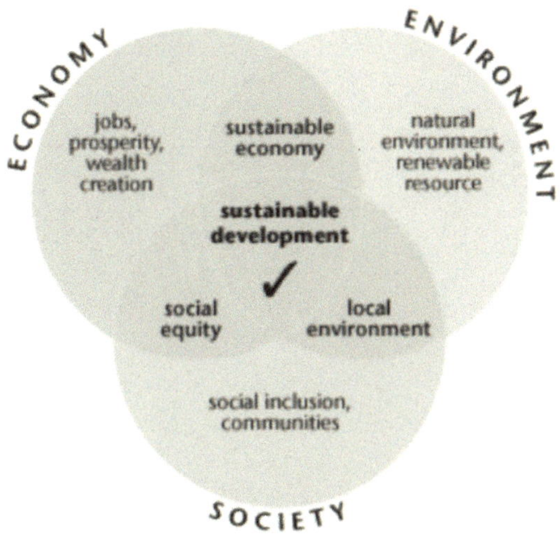

Figure 1. The Three Elements of Sustainable Development According to the British Forestry Commission

12

Strategies for Achieving SDG 12

Tae-hyun Kim

Tae-hyun Kim is the President of aSSIST(Seoul School of Integrated Sciences & Technologies) in Seoul. He received his BA in Business Administration from Yonsei University and his MA in Business Administration from Bowling Green State University. After receiving his doctorate in business administration from Indiana University, he worked as a professor at Yonsei University for over 30 years. In 2017 he was appointed president of the Seoul School of Integrated Sciences and Technologies in Seoul. His lecture interests include logistics and SCM strategy, production and operation management, operation turnaround strategy, and supply chain management strategy seminars. His research interests include supply chain strategy, production strategy, logistics and distribution strategy, and service operation strategy.

1. Introduction

Consumption and production, driving forces of global economic development, are still largely carried out through natural environment and natural resource development, a practice that tremendously deteriorates the global environment and removes places upon which future generations can rely.

According to a 2016 World Bank report, waste emissions are expected to increase by 70 percent, that is, from 2 billion tons in 2016 to 3.4 billion tons in 2050, and annual food waste accounts for about one-third of all food. Indeed, rational consumption habits should be a part of daily life. Additionally, by 2050, the world's population is expected to approach 9.6 billion, a size that will require three planets to supply the resources to support our current standard of living. Governments, businesses, and individuals face an urgent task regarding strategizing to overcome this impending crisis.

The United Nations has emphasized the need for a mindset change among people, businesses, governments, and societies in order to create a sustainable world by 2030. To this end, the United Nations launched a Sustainable Development Goal (SDG) Program in 2015 and identified 17 SDG areas, along with detailed objectives for each SDG, covering a variety of economic, social, and environmental issues. For example, they set both broad and detailed goals for SDG 1 (poverty), SDG 2 (hunger), SDG 3 (health and well-being), SDG 12 (responsible consumption and production), SDG 17 (Partnership), and so on.

The purpose of this article is to understand SDG 12, responsible consumption and production, and discuss related sustainable action strategies.

2. Key Features and Issues related to SDG 12

SDG 12 has different characteristics than other SDGs, and the practice strategy for SDG 12 is discussed based on these characteristics below.

First, the work of SDG 12 is interlinked with that of the 16 other SDGs. Therefore, decision making with regard to SDG 12 can have a positive or negative impact on performance in other SDG areas. For example, SDG 1 (poverty) and SDG 12 (responsible consumption and production) may have some negative correlation with SDG 1 objectives. Given that SDG 12 basically pursues tasks from an economic perspective, that is, energy efficient use and sustainable consumption patterns, a negative relationship with an SDG that values environment and quality of life is possible. Additionally, there are special situations in which SDG 12 issues are bound to have trade-off relationships with other SDGs in terms of decision making given that SDG 12 must also value environmental factors and satisfactory life values (Foneseca, 2020). Foneseca has shown that the work of SDG 12 is strongly correlated with that of other SDGs. Therefore, SDG 12 is often seen in trade-off situations where various criteria must be discussed.

Second, since SDG 12 concerns the interrelationship between consumption and production, various decisions must be made with respect to multi-level distribution channels, such as procurement, production, logistics, distribution, and consumption, suggesting use of supply chain management (SCM) know-how. Third, there are many participants in decision making because the processes of the supply chain are long and diverse. Since there are various players, such as consumers, manufacturers, suppliers, logistics companies, and distributors, as well as governments, NGOs, and civic groups in charge of global public affairs, strong communication skills and strong leadership are needed.

Fortunately, the detailed objective SDG 12.1 recommends that "all countries implement a 10-year planning framework for sustainable consumption and production patterns under the leadership of developed countries, taking into account the development and capabilities of developing countries." This can serve as a touchstone for SDG 12 work practice because it is an important guideline for achieving SDG 12. Considering the development and capabilities of developing countries as included in the United Nations Sustainable Development Conference (2012), developed countries are planning a 10-year period of sustainable consumption and production. The plan includes sustainable living and education, a sustainable diet, sustainable buildings and construction, and sustainable tourism, so that developing countries can promote growth without destroying the environment, and advanced countries can continue sustainable consumption and production. This protocol will serve as the basis for achieving global sustainability goals through various relationships, strategies, and implementations between and among countries and companies.

Regarding progress toward achievement of the detailed goals 12.3 and

12.5, which are "to reduce food waste by half of the world's population and loss from food production and supply chains" and "the goal of reducing waste through reuse," respectively, great progress would be made if countries and the global public try to be responsible. Currently, Korea's food waste is about 5.7 million tons, with 20 trillion won in losses; this seems to be an area where the government and consumers could realize great reduction if the task is approached with interest.

3. Introducing supply chain management for the strategic implementation of SDG 12

As mentioned above, SDG 12 overlaps many of the other SDGs' detailed objectives, so trade-off situations may occur frequently. Additionally, since consumption and production issues must be determined through various value chains, SDG12's "responsible consumption and production" field should gain excellent results through a thorough decision-making process with the introduction of the SCM methodology.

Since, as mentioned above, there is a 10-year implementation plan to achieve responsible consumption and production goals by 2030, specific measures to achieve these goals are important. Since many multi-stage distribution channels and decision makers will be involved, the following supply chain implementation strategies are needed.

First, to achieve SDG 12, we could benchmark the top-performing companies in terms of SCM (e.g., Zara, Samsung Electronics, and

Amazon) and develop an SCM system suitable for the SDG 12 environment.

Second, it is necessary to have a clear mission and operating system, which entails selecting a general manager who has experience managing the global supply chain in light of SDG 12.

Third, to manage an optimal supply chain that will satisfy needs related to the economy, the environment, and humans' quality of life, the general manager should share the managerial goal with members and unify the organization based on trust.

Fourth, the following are necessary: (1) connectivity to communicate with various members, institutions, and countries in the supply chain; (2) transparent decision making, with data or content viewing with the other party; and (3) a system for collaborative planning with the other party. In particular, assuming there are countries, companies, consumers, and NGO groups involved in achieving SDG 12, everyone should be interconnected, so that all situations may be viewed as a collective, and so that plans can be shared, if necessary, through cooperative relations across relevant parties.

Once such a system is established, SDG 12 will be achieved smoothly.

4. Conclusion

It is common for companies to approach SCM at the economic level. However, in recent years, some companies have tended to incorporate additional environmental issues in terms of sustainability or ESG management. At that level, a strategy to identify and learn from top-performing companies as a benchmark is needed.

Additionally, since many actors, such as the governments, individuals, companies, NGOs, and civic groups, are involved in the promotion of the SDGs, it is necessary to strive to form relationships including business-government, government-government, government-citizen organizations, and business-citizen organizations.

If cooperation is achieved and communication is active, these elements will contribute to achieving goals of SDG 12 and thus power a big step toward a sustainable world.

13

Climate Crisis that Can No Longer be Avoided

Seul-ah Lee

Seul-ah Lee is currently an assistant professor at the College of Life Sciences, Kyung Hee University, Korea. She obtained her PhD degree from the School of Pharmacy, Sungkyunkwan University, and continued her research as a postdoctoral researcher at Korea Polar Research Institute (KOPRI). She was an adjunct professor at Seoul School of Integrated Sciences and Technologies. She has been focusing on the chemical analysis and structural elucidation of secondary metabolites from Korean wild mushrooms, plants, Antarctic lichens and microorganisms. Her research interests include discovery of anti-cancer and anti-diabetic agents from medicinal natural products, and exploration of novel components that prevent emerging infectious diseases, predicted through the discovery of bacteria found in Antarctica due to global warming.

Recently, climate disasters have been occurring frequently around the world. Global warming is causing polar glaciers to melt at a rapid rate, which causes the gradual rise of the sea levels. Additionally, countries around the world are experiencing natural disasters including extreme temperatures, floods and droughts, typhoons, and forest fires. These extreme climatic phenomena have been occurring much more frequently in recent years. In particular, Korea has seen a record downpour unlike any other in the past 100 years, and Paris, France, had a major flood damage due to sudden downpours after suffering from severe drought. Even developed countries, which have been considered relatively safe from the climate crisis, are experiencing their worst-ever droughts, floods, wildfires, and heat waves. Due to the rapid acceleration of global warming, the climate crisis is now in a very serious condition and is worsening quickly. Climate change has become a serious problem that can no longer be deferred.

Since the Industrial Revolution, the increase in greenhouse gas emissions due to human activities interfered with the Earth's emission of energy, which soon led to global warming. Since greenhouse gases trap heat and raise the temperature of the Earth's surface, an increase in greenhouse gas emissions implies an increase in the Earth's temperature. As greenhouse gas emissions continue to increase, the average global temperature is actually rising every year—a direct and definite result of climate change. As global warming causes rise in the temperature of the Earth, the rate of evaporation of water on the ground surface increases. Consequently, the amount of water vapor present in the air increases, and this results in the increased precipitation. In fact, studies have reported that the Earth's precipitation is increasing, causing various pollutants from cities to enter rivers, which, in turn, causes the ecosystem of living things to become congested. According to a recent report, the average temperature of the Earth has risen 1.1 degrees Celsius due to global warming. To prevent a climate crisis, the Earth's temperature rise should not exceed 1.5 degrees Celsius. However, according to a report by the World Meteorological Organization (WMO) under the United Nations, there is a 50 percent chance that the Earth's average annual temperature will rise by 1.5 degrees within the next 5 years. This implies that the incidence of possible damage to be caused by global warming is also expected to increase.

According to a recent study, whereas the average area of the Arctic Sea ice in the summer season was 7.667 million square kilometers until the 1980s, it shrunk to 3.925 million square kilometers in 2020, which is only 48.9% of the original size. If this trend continues, it is predicted that the Arctic ice will no longer exist by the summer of 2030. Rising temperatures of the Earth also lead to rise in sea levels. Representative factors of sea level rise include melting polar glaciers and increasing ocean heat content. When the temperature rises, frozen freshwater melts and flows into the sea. The sea is also directly affected by temperature; that is, the temperature of the oceans rises, and the volume of seawater is affected by melted freshwater and marine warming, causing the sea level to rise, which puts many coastal cities at risk. Rising sea levels affect the coastal ecosystem, reducing the habitats and biodiversity of living organisms and leading to the loss of ecosystem functions.

Climate crisis can also cause infectious diseases. As the atmospheric temperature rises, various bacteria or germs become rampant and they may re-emerge as the permafrost melts. A few years ago, anthrax, which was officially eradicated from the Earth in the 1960s, was re-discovered in Siberia, Russia. A 12-year-old boy died, and about 20 local residents were infected due to the re-emergence of anthrax, which is known to live for more than 100 years in the frozen bodies of dead animals. Furthermore, over 2,300 reindeer were killed. Experts predicted that the infection may have occurred due to the melting of permafrost due to abnormal high temperatures, exposing the carcasses of animals infected with anthrax. Researchers at Ohio State University also found 33 virus genes in ice samples from the Tibetan Plateau glacier, which have been identified as a new type of virus that are not in the database. Global warming is increasingly likely to cause temperatures to rise and the permafrost to melt, revealing viruses of tens of thousands years-old. This trend may lead to pandemics that are more critical than the novel coronavirus (COVID-19), which still exists in our lives.

The climate crisis is, after all, an energy problem, and, as mentioned earlier, greenhouse gases are the main culprits. Earth's climate system is collapsing because of excessive greenhouse gas emissions from many different sources. It is not only human economic and industrial activities that are increasing the emissions; greenhouse gases generated in nature are also steadily increasing. This includes the rise of greenhouse gases naturally occurring in the Arctic frozen earth layer and the tundra region of Alaska due to global warming. Once released into the atmosphere, greenhouse gases remain there for a very long time; in fact, one-fifth of the greenhouse gases emitted today are said to remain in the atmosphere after 10,000 years. Carbon neutrality is the most important aspect of efforts to prevent this. “Carbon” is a shortened term for carbon dioxide, and “neutral” means being in the middle or on neither side. In a word, carbon neutrality means effectively “zero” carbon dioxide emissions, as these constitute the main culprit of global warming that causes the climate crisis. However, even if all activities that emit greenhouse gases are completely stopped, there is no realistic way to achieve a zero state. Therefore, “zero carbon” refers to the concept of reabsorbing the emitted carbon dioxide to make the actual emissions “zero.”

Climatologists are predicting five climate change scenarios caused by greenhouse gas emissions. Among them, choosing an intermediate route, which is considered the most realistic goal, the Earth’s temperature is expected to rise 2.7 degrees. This is not only over 1.5 degrees, which experts see as the threshold, it is also over 2.0 degrees, which is above the threshold to prevent climate collapse as agreed upon per the Paris Convention. With this trend, we will experience the highest average temperature in Earth’s history in the last 3 million years. A 1.0 degree rise in the Earth’s temperature would result in 50 million cases of water shortage and 300,000 deaths. When the Earth’s temperature rises 2.0 degrees, the amount of water available will decrease by 20–30%, and the sea level will rise by 7 meters. Additionally, 15–40% of the Arctic life will be endangered, and 60 million people will be exposed to malaria. If the Earth’s temperature rises 3.0 degrees, coastal flooding will damage 160 million people per year, famine will kill 3 million people, 20–50% of living organisms will be endangered, and the Amazon rainforest will be destroyed.

The Intergovernmental Panel on Climate Change (IPCC) declared that global carbon dioxide emissions must be reduced by at least 45% by 2030 compared to 2010, and carbon neutrality must be achieved by 2050, in order to limit the global temperature increase to less than 1.5 degrees by 2100. If the average temperature increase is targeted at 2.0 degrees, carbon dioxide emissions should be reduced by about 25% by 2030 compared to 2010, and carbon neutrality should be achieved by 2070. Countries such as Sweden, Britain, France, Denmark, New Zealand, and Hungary have already enacted carbon neutrality, and major countries in Europe as well as China and Japan have declared carbon neutrality goals. Additionally, U.S. President Joe Biden rejoined the Paris Agreement shortly after taking office and promised to achieve carbon neutrality by 2050.

Thus far, we have been passive in responding to climate change, but now, we are confronted with a serious crisis that we can no longer escape. Climate change and abnormal climate phenomena are causing extensive damage around the world. In response, U.S. President Biden is reportedly considering declaring a climate emergency. Our daily lives are very closely related to global warming. To slow down the acceleration of global warming even minimally, we must implement small efforts toward low-carbon living. It is necessary to reduce the use of private cars in favor of public transportation or walking and to maintain an appropriate temperature when using air conditioners. To reduce waste, it is necessary to reduce the use of disposable products, cook mindfully, and adopt the habit of using reusable shopping carriers instead of plastic bags. These measures are commonsensical; everyone is aware of them, but some people believe that their small effort may not contribute to changing the world.

However, we should remember that our individual efforts can be a starting point for global change. It is my hope that small daily-life habits will contribute to achieving carbon neutrality by 2050.

14

SDGs for a Clean Ocean Environment and Ocean Space Utilization

Jong-gye Shin

Dr. Jong-gye Shin is a chair professor at aSSIST(Seoul School of Integrated Sciences & Technologies) in Seoul, South Korea. He received his Ph.D. degree from M.I.T.(Massachusetts Institute of Technology) in U.S.A. He is a professor emeritus at Seoul National University where he was a professor for 27 years. Currently, he works as a technology advisor at Korea Shipbuilding and Offshore Engineering, the world largest shipbuilding group. His specialty is ship production system, shipbuilding business strategy, and maritime digitalization. He is the only three-time winner of the Elmer Hann award for the best paper in ship production from Society of Naval Architects and Marine Engineers, U.S.A.

1. Introduction

The ocean, which accounts for about 70 percent of the Earth's surface, is a treasure trove of human food, energy, and resources. The ocean absorbs carbon dioxide from the atmosphere and supplies oxygen. It also absorbs more than 90 percent of the Earth's heat energy, which has increased due to global warming, and circulates with the ocean currents in order to heat and cool the atmosphere and control the planet's climate. The ocean, however, is constantly being polluted. Marine waste, rising water temperatures and sea level due to global warming, and the pollution of fish and shellfish are becoming serious.

The value of the ocean is infinite. For the sake of humanity, the marine environment must be simultaneously preserved and utilized. The ocean is a wide, deep, and unknown space. The limitations of existing science and technology may be overcome through the study of creatures in the ocean. Just as spacecraft are needed for space exploration, marine conservation and utilization require various floating structures and underwater vehicles, such as ships, offshore plants, submarines, multi-functional marine cities, and thus related technologies must be developed. It is necessary to establish long-term and fundamental goals and implement plans specifically for the conservation and utilization of sustainable oceans.

2. Issues for marine pollution and utilization

Scientists predict that sea levels will rise by about 1.1 meters by 2100 due to global warming. This will flood about 2.4 billion people or 30 percent of the world's population, countries, and cities. Carbon is the main culprit of global warming. The International Maritime Organization (IMO) has created regulations to reduce greenhouse gases (GHGs), including carbon.

The ocean is constantly being polluted. Many of the land's unpurified waste and pollutants accumulate in the ocean. For instance, radioactive water from Fukushima, Japan will be released into the ocean over the next 30 years. Marine waste is emerging as an international issue, and international discussions are underway in the forum of the International Maritime Organization's Maritime Environment Protection Committee (IMOMEPC). In Korea, The Basic Plan for Marine Waste Management (2021-2030) was announced in May 2021, and pre-cycle management will be strengthened to prevent marine waste through proper waste collection and disposal.

In particular, marine pollution caused by microplastic is becoming a serious issue. According to a study by Australia's Commonwealth Scientific and Industrial Research Organisation (CSIRO), 99.8 percent of all seabirds will eat microplastic in ocean by 2050. Since marine microplastic ultimately enters the human body through fish, new technologies to remove marine microplastic are needed.

Marine pollution caused by the movement of ships, which facilitate

80 percent of world trade, is also increasing. Carbon emitted by ships sailing through the ocean accounts for about 3 percent of the world's total carbon emissions, necessitating new eco-friendly ships. Additionally, the underwater noise from ships generate adversely affects the survival of aquatic life. Specifically, noise has a negative effect on the intercommunication and breeding activities of marine mammals, and the stress from noise causes behavioral disorders in marine life, as well as population reduction. For this reason, the IMO has acknowledged marine noise as pollution and has plans to regulate it. For instance, there will be no ambient noise from future vessels.

Since the ocean is a repository of energy, food, and resources, marine space should be widely utilized. Creating renewable energy that generates electricity using offshore wind, waves, and tidal currents; securing new food for mankind through fisheries; developing new drugs using marine life; developing oil, gas, and mineral resources on the seabed; and developing marine cities are all components of the effort. Various marine structures such as ships, offshore plants, and marine cities that support marine utilization will be designed, constructed upon, installed and operated, respectively, to prevent marine pollution.

3. Cases for a future ship and ocean lives

With reference to the solutions mentioned in the previous chapter, examples of future ships and new marine life are introduced in this chapter.

Currently, in traditional ship engines, fuel is injected into the engine to drive the propeller with the force generated by combustion in the engine. In this process, carbon is emitted, and noise is generated.

From a fuel perspective, carbon-neutral fuels that can replace existing ship fuel (HFO) are needed to reduce GHGs. Liquefied natural gas (LNG), which is drawing attention as a clean fuel, can reduce GHGs by about 20 percent compared to the previous one, but it emits carbon dioxide. Methanol has the problem of incurring excessive cost in the process of collecting carbon dioxide required for the production process.

Carbon-neutral fuels include biofuels, hydrogen, and ammonia. Biofuels can technically be used immediately because they are compatible with existing propulsion methods and fuel oil, but production costs are high, and energy efficiency is low. Hydrogen has a high mass energy density, but there are limitations of low volume energy density and the necessity of cryogenic storage at -253°C. Ammonia can be mass-produced and is easy to store and transport, so it is economical compared to other carbon-neutral fuels, but if leaked, it may cause toxic damage. According to the International Energy Agency (IEA), the proportion of ammonia used is expected to gradually expand, more so than hydrogen, replacing the fuel in more than 60% of newly built ships by 2060.

To realize eco-friendly ships, it is necessary to improve the engine or use a ship battery. Until now, engines have relied on the combustion of diesel fuel, but engine design must be improved to accommodate the use of carbon-neutral fuel, and GHG emissions must be reduced through the use of batteries or fuel cells. There is also a need for technology to reduce the GHGs ships emit through the utilization of auxiliary means such as solar heat and wind power using sails.

The ship's propulsion system should be gradually converted from the current mechanical propulsion system to an electric propulsion system. A new propeller concept or propulsion system should be developed to reduce fuel consumption and emissions, and marine noise should be drastically reduced.

There are unusual creatures in the sea. Planariidae are marine life that never die, and research on the non-death enzyme is underway because planariidae regenerate their skin, intestines, and brain independently. Additionally, Thermococcus onnurineus NA1, a marine microorganism found 1,500 meters under the sea, consumes carbon monoxide and emits hydrogen. Therefore, research is exploring using this organism for hydrogen production. Many more interesting organisms can be found among marine life that can, for example, withstand high water pressure, and there are creatures that can propel themselves underwater using soft movements. There are far more unexplained creatures in the unknown ocean, so discovery and research are expected to go beyond existing science to shed light on the future of mankind.

4. SDGs for marine protection and utilization

The SDGs should promote oceans in two development directions: preservation of the marine environment and space utilization. Regarding conservation of the marine environment, there are two directions for implementation: suppression of the discharge of marine waste and management of discharged waste. Suppression of marine waste emissions should be enacted and enforced through agreements between countries and regulations issued by the United Nations. Wastes must be collected and removed from the site of generation, whether on land or at sea. For example, where carbon is emitted, equipment for collecting carbon should be installed. Microplastic inflow into the ocean should also be collected and removed where it is produced. Technology for moving collected carbon to and storing it in the sea is also being studied.

Waste that enters the ocean destroys the ecosystem. Technology to collect and remove microplastic from the ocean is needed. IMOMEPC continues to tighten regulations to reduce microplastic in the ocean, and Japanese companies such as NYK are conducting marine microplastic collection and analysis using ships, but to restore the contaminated environment, it is necessary to actually remove the microplastic. In addition to microplastics, various other marine pollutants should be collected and removed.

The utilization of marine space should be promoted in consideration of eco-friendliness. Ships in charge of maritime transport and offshore plants for acquiring subsea resources should be improved to protect the environment. Technologies that facilitate various vehicles for operating in marine spaces, such as underwater robots and underwater drones, should be developed to explore the deep-sea bottom. Wind, tidal, and wave systems for obtaining energy from the ocean should be developed and installed.

Ships operating in the ocean must use eco-friendly fuel or batteries. Although the use of LNG fuels, which are currently recognized as clean fuels, has resulted in a 20 percent reduction in GHG emissions, it is necessary to develop ship battery technologies using hydrogen, with the aim of ultimately zeroing carbon emission. There is also a need for a ship propulsion device that minimizes the generation of water sound that causes disturbance in the marine ecosystem.

The development of smart marine cities to utilize wide and deep marine spaces will be accelerated. Energy used in marine cities shall be carbon neutral and no waste is generated. Marine cities aim for an innovative high-tech functional system that can achieve self-sufficient energy, food, and water. Marine cities must utilize wind, solar, and small modular reactor for their clean energy system. A seawater desalination system will be useful and advanced communication infrastructure using satellite system, artificial intelligence, big data, and mobility. A marine city is a base station in the ocean that acts like a base station in space, and marine cities must be installed both close to the land and also far away, with functions such as airports, ports, and logistics storage.

A schematic of these sustainable objectives related to the ocean is shown in Figure 1.

Figure 1. Direction for marine conservation and utilization

5. Conclusion

The reason it is necessary to utilize marine space while preserving clean oceans is that human food, energy, and resources are obtained from the ocean. To preserve the marine environment, which is increasingly being affected by accelerating global warming and marine pollution, marine space should be utilized for the collection, recycling, and permanent storage of pollutants and wastes.

Ships, offshore plants, and underwater moving vehicles necessary for the utilization of marine space should be developed in an eco-friendly manner, and marine cities that will serve as hubs for the utilization of marine space should be designed and promoted. Various efforts are needed to secure ocean energy and the marine creatures mankind needs.

Conservation and utilization of the oceans are indispensable to human existence.

15

Society in Harmony with Nature

Yeo-chang Youn

Yeo-chang Youn is an Emirates Professor of Seoul National University (SNU) where he taught ecological economics and environmental management until 2021 and professor at aSSIST(Seoul School of Integrated Sciences & Technologies) in Seoul. He graduated University of Washington (Seattle) with PhD in forest resources and holds a BS and MS in forestry from Seoul National University, Korea. He was a founding director of interdisciplinary undergraduate program in Global Environmental Management at SNU. He is currently the Director of Institute for Sustainable Social Ecological Systems which is a research organization working on the sustainability of natural resources. He also serves as the President of Friends of Mountain and Nature, a nature conservation civil society in Korea. His research interests include economics of ecosystem services and business model for sustainable bio economy.

15.1 Biodiversity Loss

As technology has developed and trade has increased due to the influence of industrialization over the past 200 years, there have been major changes in population growth and land use in various parts of the world. As a result, the biosphere on Earth has almost no part without direct or indirect impacts, and many species have disappeared. Species that lived in the biosphere destroyed by human overuse have lost their habitat, and as a result, many species are in danger of disappearing or extinction. For example, amphibious reptiles are at risk of disappearing about a quarter. (See Figure 1)

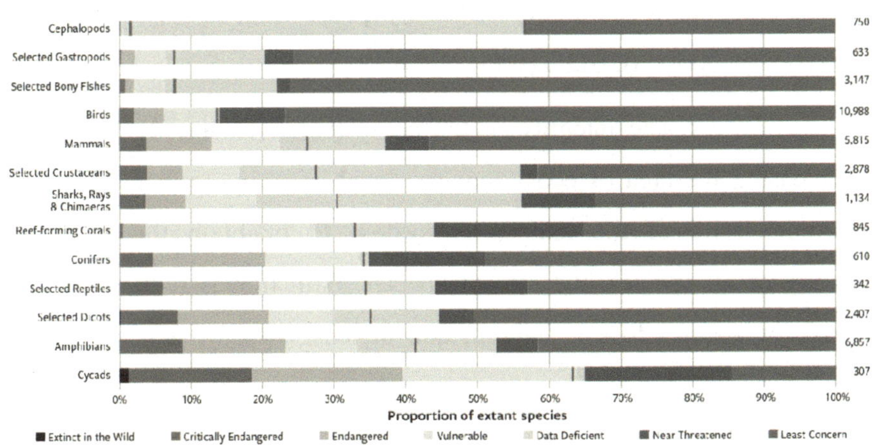

Figure 1. Percentage of existing species at risk

Species are classified by class (Sanho Exception), EW - Extinct in the Wild, CR - Critically Endangered, EN - Endangered, VU - Vulnerable, NT - Near Threatened, DD - Data Defensive, LC - Least Concern. (Source: The IUCN Red List of Threatened Species 2022)

The degree of risk of extinction varies according to species. Specifically, 69% of small irons, 41% of amphibian reptiles, 34% of conifers, 33% of coral, 27% of mammals, and 13%m of birds are at risk.

To solve the problem of the loss of biodiversity on Earth, UN member states gathered in Rio de Janeiro, Brazil in 1992 and agreed to prevent the loss of biodiversity. In order to implement the UN Convention on Biological Diversity, the Nagoya Protocol was adopted in 2010 in Nagoya, Japan, and the Aichi targets were set. However, most of the Aichi targets have not been achieved. (Secretariat of the Convention on Biological Diversity, 2021). In order to implement the UN Convention on the Conservation of Biodiversity, each country has to set four goals to reflect the value of biodiversity in its economic system and maintain ecosystem services essential to all human lives by preserving, restoring and using it wisely by 2050. (CBD 2021)

OBJECTIVE A: The integrity of the ecosystem is enhanced. To this end, by increasing the area of ecosystem protected areas by 15% and increasing the connectivity of the natural ecosystem to maintain the health and elasticity of all species, the rate of species extinction is reduced by 1/10, the risk of species loss is halved, and at least 90% of genetic diversity is maintained.

OBJECTIVE B: Through conservation and sustainable use of biodiversity, the benefits of nature are properly evaluated, and biodiversity contributes to sustainable development.

OBJECTIVE C: Benefits from the use of genetic resources are fairly shared and contribute to the sustainable use and conservation of biodiversity.

OBJECTIVE D: There will be no difference in the availability of financial and other enforcement measures necessary to achieve the vision of creating a world in harmony with nature between developing and developed countries.

15.2 Sustainable Use of Ecosystems and Ecosystem Services

The use of sustainable ecosystems is necessary to prevent biodiversity loss. When ecosystems are used in a way that guarantees biodiversity conservation, nature can provide various services to mankind. These natural benefits are called ecosystem services. Nature, human well being, and ecosystem services are changed by human behavior, human made artificial environment, and social systems. If this relationship is schematized, it can be expressed as shown in Figure 2.

Ecosystem services can be divided into four main categories: material services that provide materials, services that regulate the environment, cultural services, and services that support life. These four ecosystem services are directly related to our well-being by affecting safety, supply of daily necessities, health, maintaining social relationships, and freedom of choice. (See Figure 3)

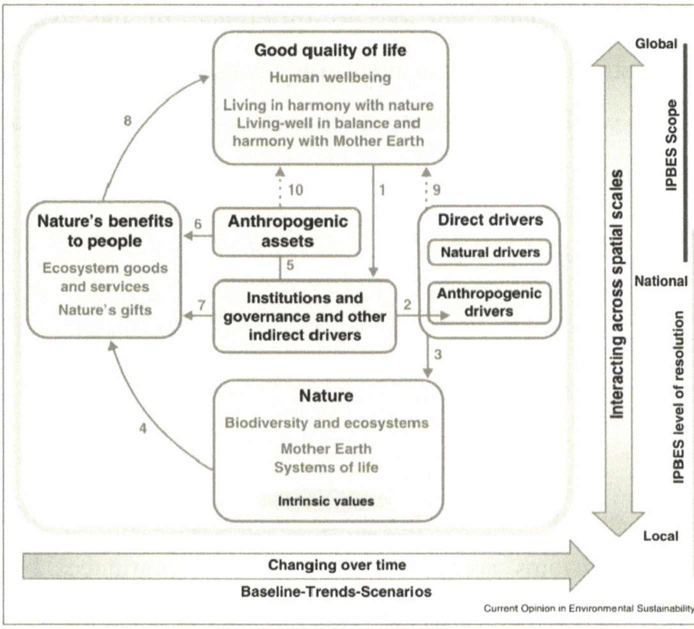

Figure 2. Human Behavior and Nature, Ecosystem Services, and Human Well-being: Spatial Relationships(source: Sandra Díaz etl at. 2015)

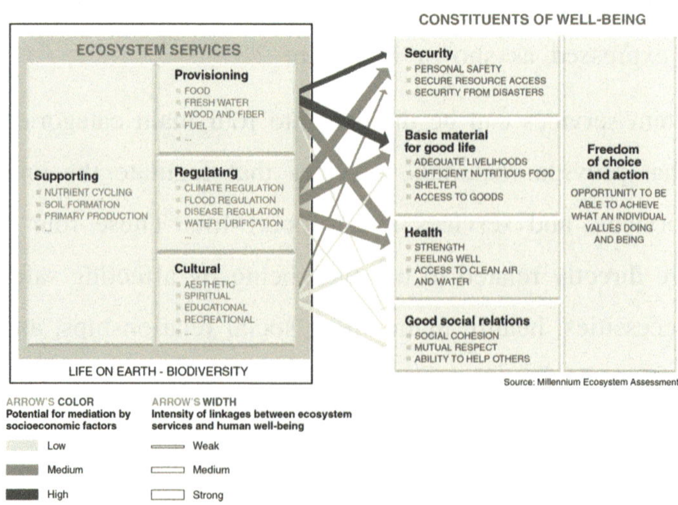

Figure 3. Ecosystem services and human well-being

Sustainable use of the ecosystem means using the ecosystem so that ecosystem services can be supplied sustainably. Specifically, it refers to the use of land and aquatic ecosystems so that various lives can be harmonized together on Earth. It is necessary for operation of agriculture, forestry, and fisheries industries such that creatures living in forests, farmland, rivers and lakes can sustain their life. In addition, environmental pollutants emitted by urban society into the atmosphere, soil, and sewers should be restricted to prevent ecosystems such as forests, farmland, rivers, and lakes from losing their original nature. In order for the ecosystem to maintain its original state, biodiversity must be preserved. Many countries including South Korea have introduced legal and financial policy instruments. For example, the Biodiversity Protection Act was enacted in South Korea introduced policy measures such as 1) expanded protected areas, 2) restriction of use of biological resources, and 3) payment for ecosystem services for the conservation of biodiversity.

15.3 Human Society Symbiosis with Nature

In order for our society to move further into a sustainable society, fundamental social change is needed in the following six areas. 1) Expanding educational opportunities and eliminating gender inequality, 2) Social mechanisms to protect public health, 3) Carbon neutral energy conversion, 4) Food, land, water, and marine ecosystems management, 5) Solving urban problems, 6) Digital transformation.

Among these transformations, health, energy, food and water, and urban society are directly or indirectly related to the use and preservation of the ecosystem. Without the health of the ecosystem, human health cannot be guaranteed. Energy conversion to the use of ecosystem-based carbon neutral energy that can sustainable industrial development is required. Land should be used to enable sustainable supply of food and water, and urban green areas should be expanded to create an ecologically healthy city.

Currently, 8.6% of the world's population (1.4 billion people, as of 2018) suffers from hunger and malnutrition with income of less than $1.25 a day (UN Statistic), and 13% of adults become obese with excessive intake. The emission of greenhouse gases due to poor land use and a wasteful food culture accounts for a quarter of the total greenhouse gas emissions on Earth, causing the loss of biodiversity and water and air pollution. Since the food production system is very vulnerable to climate change, the food production and consumption system, land use, and marine resource management should be comprehensively reorganized to cope with climate change. However, land use, marine and agricultural policies are very complexly related, making it difficult to establish and implement policies for integrated transformation. Due to these characteristics, it is difficult to agree on the establishment of global biodiversity goals for land use and marine management agreed internationally. Currently, a proposal has been submitted to expand the protected area to 30% of the Earth's surface area to preserve biodiversity by 2030. Except for the expansion of the protected area, realistic policy indicators have not been developed for the transformation of the food production and consumption system, land use, and marine resource management. (UN. 2022)

References

Secretariat of the Convention on Biological Diversity (2020) Global Biodiversity Outlook 5 – Summary for Policy Makers. Montréal.

CBD. First draft of the post-2020 global biodiversity framework. OPEN ENDED WORKING GROUP ON THE POST-2020 GLOBAL BIODIVERSITY FRAMEWORK Third meeting. Online, 23 August – 3 September 2021. Item 4 of the provisional agenda
https://www.iucnredlist.org/resources/summary-statistics

Millennium Ecosystem Assessment, 2005. Ecosystems and Human Well-being: Synthesis. Island Press, Washington, DC.

UN. 2022. Sustainable Development Goals Report.
https://unstats.un.org/sdgs/dataportal/

Sandra Dı´az etl at. 2015. The IPBES Conceptual Framework – connecting nature and people. Current Opinion in Environmental Sustainability 14: 1-15. Elsevier.

16

Strategies for Creating a Sustainable Brand

Dal-ju Mun

Strategies for Creating a Sustainable Brand

Dal-ju Mun is an associate professor at aSSIST(Seoul School of Integrated Sciences & Technologies) in Seoul. He was awarded a PhD in marketing from PARIS IIIV University, France. He served as the head of the ORICOM Brand Strategy Research Center and a member of the Government Innovation Brand Committee. He has been giving lectures on brand marketing at numerous companies and has been consulting and advising on corporate brand marketing.

1. Introduction

In corporate management, profit seeking has traditionally been the most important factor. However, in the 2000s, the concept of sustainable management emerged, and the era when companies only needed to be profitable ended. The trend of consumers researching how companies make money (content) and how much they do for the good of the world (impact) before making purchases is growing. As stories about Ottogi have spread (the company has 99% full-time employees; win-win growth, with suppliers who pay the price of goods; has helped 4,358 children with heart disease over 25 years; provides financial support for surgery; has spent 4 billion in private funds on scholarships over 21 years and 150 billion in inheritance tax sincere payment), the company acquired the nickname Gottogi, which is a combination of God and Ottogi, and there was even a movement among consumers promoting the purchase of Ottogi products. Present-day consumers do not praise companies simply for making good products; an increasing number of people are asking whether companies are sincerely fulfilling their social responsibilities. In terms of corporate growth, whereas financial factors such as sales and net profit were previously paramount, now, both financial factors and the company's social influence are important.

As climate change, environmental problems, greenhouse gases, and social problems have become more serious, companies can only survive in the long run in the current era by honoring all the relevant social, environmental, and economic considerations. Therefore, environmental, social, and governance (ESG) and Sustainable Development Goals (SDGs) are the keywords that are attracting the most attention in corporate management these days. ESG refers to the management of a transparent and fair governance structure by assuming social responsibility as a company, without destroying the environment, toward long-term return growth and sustainable growth of the company. The SDGs are common to humanity and must be achieved by 2030, per the United Nations' 2015 declaration, in order to address issues such as poverty reduction, inequality, job creation, economic growth, and climate change. The idea of pursuing sustainability is complementary. From a company's viewpoint, ESG is an activity toward achieving the SDGs, and the SDGs are the criteria for ESG evaluation. Hence, present-day corporate strategies are evolving into ESGSDG integration strategies. Investors and consumers judge "how well companies make money" (financial strategy), but they also judge "how companies make money" (ESG) and "how companies contribute to society" (SDGs).

2. Changes in the reasons for a company's existence

Responsible consumption is on the rise. According to the Trend Monitor 2019 survey, 78% of individuals agreed that buying an item nowadays requires conceptual consumption. According to the Korea Chamber of Commerce and Industry's 2022 MZ Generation survey, 64.5% of individuals indicated that they would purchase products from companies that demonstrate best practices regarding ESG, even if the products are expensive. In current times, it is common for cosmetics companies to display information on product containers claiming that their products have not been tested on animals. This is not because companies love animals but rather because a large proportion of consumers are animal lovers, including dog owners, who share stories about cruel animal testing in connection with certain products.

The case of the Disney movie *Mulan* depicts how important consumers are to ESGSDG management, as consumers boycotted the movie after learning that the lead actor, Liu Yifei, supported police suppression of the Hong Kong protests and that the movie was filmed in the Uighur mountain lodge region, a controversial area regarding human rights oppression. Consequently, the intended blockbuster *Mulan*, in which $100 million had been invested, earned only $66 million in profits due to the global boycott.

In contemporary times, the reason for companies' existence has changed. In the past, money-making methods and the type of business one should pursue were important. However, now we have to think more deeply about why we do business. Resultantly, non-financial factors such as environmental concerns, social responsibility, and governance have naturally grown in importance. The world has become one where it is important which company makes what, with what intention, and with how much sincerity.

3. ESGSDG activities from a brand perspective

Recently, many companies have adopted solving social and environmental problems as their main direction and are conducting related marketing and public relations activities. However, no companies are particularly noteworthy in this regard. This is because many companies are using environmental marketing simply as a means to stimulate consumption. On the other hand, many companies view ESGSDG strategies as ethical or mandatory, but there is no differentiation between companies. However, if companies want to internalize ESGSDG as the center of their business activities, they need to approach it from the perspective of branding. Branding is an activity that truly conveys the purpose and core values of the brand as customer value. Companies should incorporate ESGSDG in their brand strategy, so that ESGSDG naturally becomes an essential element of all the management activities the company implements. Hence, employees will naturally think and act accordingly in their respective roles. This seems to be the reason underlying Pulmuone employees' superior performance, as well as Yuhan-Kimberly employees' stronger tendency to work with the environment in mind.

ESGSDG should move toward capturing customer value in the context of the company's brand. Unilever's Lipton tea is an exemplar case in which the customer value of a product and ESGSDG activities are well linked in corporate branding activities. Generally, the tea market is characterized by unit price battles to generate considerable profit compared to the production costs, so there is little differentiation in terms of customer value. However, Unilever has created a value that differs significantly from that of existing tea brands through a brand campaign with the slogan "You can change the world by drinking a cup of tea." Their value differentiation succeeded because of initiatives that improved the working environment on tea farms and the treatment of workers, while also covering the tuition expenses of workers' children. As positive word of mouth spread, both the market share and sales of Unilever tea increased.

According to Thomas Kloster, CEO of Goodverting, to create a sustainable brand, "The public nature of a company must reflect its social responsibility, and it must lead to substantial competitiveness in its operations and key management activities for sustainability."

4. How to create a sustainable brand

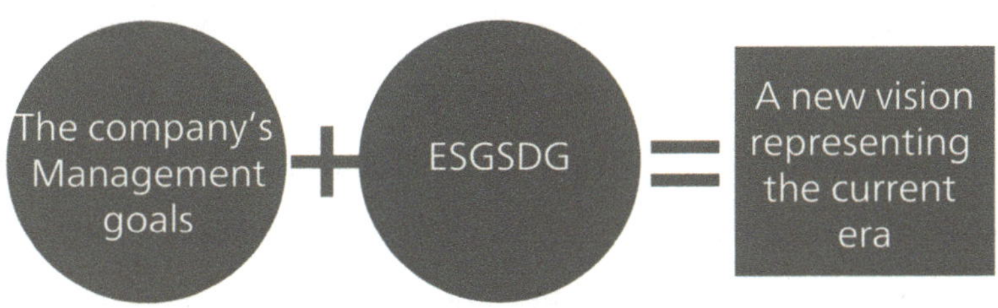

Figure 1. Establishing a new vision centered on ESGSDG

For a company to create a sustainable brand, it is necessary to set the company's vision and goals from the perspective of ESGSDG, then establish strategies, tasks, and execution systems to achieve these goals, and promote them consistently.

First, a company must establish a new vision centered on ESGSDG in line with the trend of the current era.

All companies already have their own management goals. Companies must now build a new vision that represents the current era by incorporating ESGSDG into their existing management goals. Generally, successful companies have grown with society, with the philosophy and purpose of providing products and services that consumers of the relevant era need. In the early 1900s, for example, Henry Ford realized his dream by making cars that fulfilled many people's desire to move farther, faster, and more freely.

Today, new markets and growth opportunities are emerging for companies willing to integrate the ESGSDG strategy, which helps with understanding consumers' crisis-conscious behavior regarding the sustainability of the planet and society and allows consumers to practice sustainable living more smoothly and easily. According to Jeon Min-gu, executive director of Sustainable Brands Korea, "We make the best products but do not cause unnecessary environmental damage, and [we] use business to form [a] consensus on environmental crises and implement solutions." A good example is Patagonia's corporate philosophy and business purpose. Moreover, Lotte Chemical, which represents Korea's chemical material industry, has acknowledged the seriousness of the environmental problems mankind is facing and responded in May 2022 with the new vision "Every Step for Green," which alludes to leading the development of technologies to cope with carbon neutrality. The first step in creating a sustainable brand is incorporating the ESGSDG strategy into the company's philosophy and purpose of existence to redefine the corporate philosophy and business purpose in line with the preoccupations of this era.

Second, it is necessary to choose specific campaign topics to create an appropriate ESGSDG image for the company.

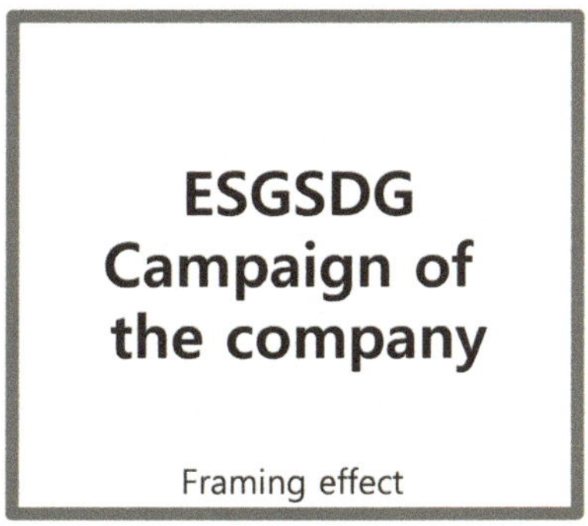

Figure 2. Select a specific campaign theme

In contemporary times, many companies spend considerable amounts of money to become leaders in ESGSDG management, and they create various content as part of marketing and promotion strategies. However, there are no particularly memorable companies in this regard. To differentiate companies, a unique frame of persuasion is needed. Companies need to think about how to plant their own differentiated ESGSDG image in the minds of customers. To do so, it is necessary to select a specific campaign topic to create the ESGDG image that the company wants. The company's brand should be seen within the framework that the company pursues. To achieve this, companies should share the desired direction with consumers. This is the framing effect.

SPC Group Paris Baguette has, since September 2020, continuously practiced helping local farmers suffering due to the effects of the novel coronavirus (COVID-19) pandemic under the campaign theme "ESG Happiness: A Win-Win Project." It is continuing its win-win journey by introducing products that utilize potatoes from Pyeongchang, Gangwon Province, Jeju Gujwa, strawberries from Nonsan in Chungnam, onions from Muan in Jeollanam-do, and ginsengs from Punggi in Yeongju, Gyeongsangbuk-do. Additionally, Market Kurly launched a campaign under the theme "ALL Paper Challenge" and changed all its packaging to entirely paper packaging, resulting in 4,831 tons of plastic savings over a year. Specifically, Styrofoam boxes have been replaced by paper boxes, vinyl paper pouches have replaced zippered bags, paper tape is now used to tape boxes, and vinyl buffer packaging materials have been replaced by paper buffer packaging materials.

Third, it is imperative to continuously practice the chosen theme with sincerity.

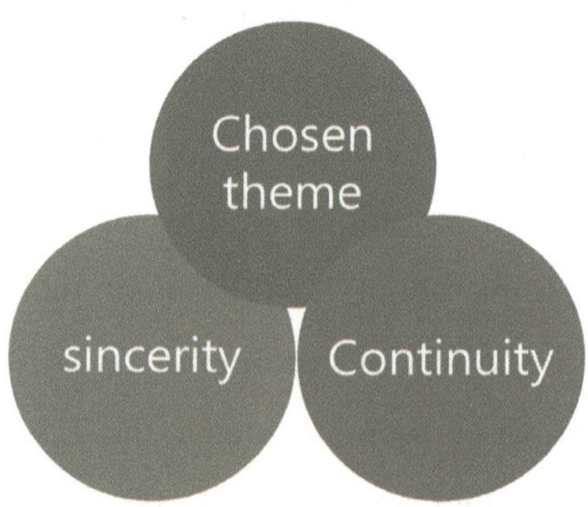

Figure 3. Be sincere and continue to practice in line with the chosen theme

The ESGSDG-centered branding strategy incurs costs in the short term, but in the mid- to long term, it should be viewed as an investment that can improve the value of the company and reduce future costs. To achieve this, it is necessary to have patience and continue to practice with sincerity.

Starbucks is conducting a "Better Together, Value Together" campaign as part of its ESGSDG marketing. Having started with "Better Together Eco-Friendly," which entails using eco-friendly products such as paper straws and minimizing the use of disposable products, the campaign has expanded to "Better Together Planet," with the aim of reducing carbon by 30%, and "Better Together People," which focuses on hiring local talent. This campaign is Starbucks' mid- to long-term strategy; it encompasses ESGSDG activities and plays a central role in projecting the image of ESGSDG management. The common characteristic of companies that have successfully built an ESGSDG management image is that they all selected a specific campaign topic, showed sincerity, continuously executed the campaigns, and then expanded them.

5. Conclusion

Due to the COVID-19 pandemic as well as various abnormal climatic events such as droughts and floods, the call for companies to demonstrate environmental and social responsibility is mounting. From the perspective of companies, ESGSDG practice is becoming profitable, not costly. If a company adopts sustainable management, which fulfills social responsibility, the company's credit rating will rise, making it easier to attract investment, reducing capital-raising costs, improving the corporate image, increasing demand for products, and increasing profits. Therefore, leading global companies are already actively using ESGSDG as an opportunity for new growth engines. It is time for Korean companies to adopt ESGSDG as a growth engine that can create new opportunities, not just for risk management purposes. For companies to create a sustainable brand, they need patience with the strategic application process, to set a vision and goals in line with the ESGSDG perspective, and to select specific campaign topics for the company to create the desired image, and to ensure continuous implementation accordingly.

17

Global Partnership*

Jeong-ho Pyo

* This article is based on various data released by the United Nations

Jeong-ho Pyo is a chair professor at aSSIST(Seoul School of Integrated Sciences & Technologies) in Seoul. He was awarded a PhD from Seoul National University and bachelor's degree from Korea University Business School in Seoul, South Korea. He was a professor of SoonChunHyang University in Asan, South Korea. He is retired now and is serving as an honorary professor. He has been researching, teaching and consulting in the broad area of International Business and Strategy, Foreign direct investment of Korean companies, Corporate ecological structure innovation, Internationalization of Korean small and medium-sized enterprises (SMEs). Especially recently, he is interested in AI-based Business Innovation and Digital Transformation.

1. Introduction

Partnership refers to an agreement to cooperate with each other to increase mutual benefit. Therefore, the most important aspect of partnership is to build mutual trust in terms of keeping an agreement with each other, and to achieve this, it must be a win-win relationship for both parties. The relationship cannot endure if only one side helps the other or receives help from the other. This is especially true in global relations with large political, economic, and cultural gaps.

Fortunately, globalization is deepening day by day with the development of transportation and communication technologies, and the global village is transforming into a closer-knit neighborhood. However, problems that cannot be easily solved without global corporation, such as climate change and other environmental problems, the population and food supply problem, the fine dust problem, the economic polarization and inequality problem, are accumulating. Therefore, the global village has now reached a stage where it is difficult to even survive without cooperation; hence, global partnership has become an essential virtue of the global village. For this reason, It is indeed timely and meaningful that the United Nations (UN) has recently emphasized global partnership for the achievement of the SDGs.

Global partnership was first raised at the UN Millennium Summit in 2000 as an implementation method to effectively promote the UN's development agenda. The UN Summit also emphasized the establishment of partnerships among various actors including the private sector, non-governmental organizations, and civil society, and the 2014 UN General Assembly resolution "Towards a global partnership" brought focus to stakeholders who can share and mobilize knowledge, skills, and financial resources. Such partnership has been recommended for developing countries as a driving force for achieving the post-2015 development agenda.

The SDGs comprise the agenda the UN advocated at the 70th summit held in 2015 and refer to 17 global economic, social, and environmental goals to be achieved by 2030. Among them, SDG 17 aims to strengthen the means of implementation as well as global partnerships to achieve all the SDGs. SDG 17 consists of 19 specific goals, which are broadly divided into six categories: financial resources, technology, capacity building, trade, maintaining the stability and consistency of policies and systems, various stakeholder partnerships, data availability, and strengthening statistical capabilities. Therefore, in this paper, we would like to review the detailed goals for each sector and the progress and issues so far and suggest improvement plans.

2. Detailed objectives, progress, and key issues for each sector

2.1 The financial sector

This section aims to strengthen international support for tax and public revenue collection in developing countries as well as support such as debt relief and debt adjustment, achieve a 0.7% official development assistance (ODA) to gross national income (GNI) ratio in developed countries, and introduce and implement investment promotion systems in the poorest countries.

To prepare financial resources for development cooperation in developing countries, it is necessary to first strengthen the capacity of developing countries to mobilize domestic financial resources by improving their ability to collect taxes and other forms of public revenue. For this, it is necessary to reorganize the tax system, implement efficient tax collection, and strengthen efforts to prevent tax evasion. Next, The detailed objective of SDG 17 stipulates that advanced countries will fulfill their ODA commitments, aiming to achieve a 0.7% ODA to GNI ratio and mobilizing financial resources for development in developing countries as well as overseas direct investment, green bonds, and carbon credits. SDG 17 also encourages the mobilization of public and private capital through various innovative methods such as the transaction system, supports developing countries' debt repayment capacity, and proposes debt relief to alleviate the debt burden of poor and high-debt countries. In particular, for the least developed countries, it specifies an investment promotion plan to support the achievement of a GDP growth rate of at least 7% per annum and an investment-to-GDP ratio of at least 25%.

However, despite these detailed targets, the commitment to a 0.7% ODA ratio in developed countries is not being well kept; for example, in Korea, this ratio was only 0.14% as of 2020. Furthermore, the financial dearth as an obstacle to achieving the SDGs by 2030 has risen to 4.2 trillion won, but some countries, including the United Kingdom and

Norway, are moving to reduce ODA. Various methods for mobilizing financial resources, such as debt relief for the least developed countries, maintaining the minimum GDP growth rate, and achieving the minimum investment ratio, are not realized due to the lack of active private participation, necessitating more systematic efforts.

2.2 The technical cooperation sector

In this sector, the detailed goals include strengthening inter-Korean, South–South, triangular, regional, and international cooperation in science and technology and innovation, with particular attention to the development and transfer of technology under favorable conditions to/for developing countries and the spread of appropriate technology such as ICT to the least developed countries.

SDG 17 aims to strengthen scientific, technological, and innovative cooperation amongst countries and expand knowledge sharing. The UN has long established UNCTAD to promote South–South cooperation. The UN has also created a special organization to promote technological cooperation amongst developing countries. Additionally, the UN has been making efforts to develop for, transfer to, and utilize clean and eco-friendly technologies in developing countries, especially the least developed countries, and strengthen the operation of technology banks and technology capacity-strengthening mechanisms, alongside the utilization of implementation technologies.

However, these detailed goals have been limited in terms of actual implementation. This is because true technological cooperation can be achieved through inter-Korean cooperation rather than South-South cooperation, as the latter is difficult in the era of technological competition among countries and companies. However, since general technology related to people's livelihood is sufficient for inter-Korean cooperation in terms of technical aid, systematic efforts are required.

2.3 Developing countries' capacity-building sectors

The UN believes that the ability of developing countries to achieve sustainable development is largely determined by their ecological and geographical conditions as well as by their national institutions. Hence, the UN has emphasized the importance of competency development and international cooperation to support developing countries.

Regardless of how much help or cooperation is given, it is difficult to achieve the desired effect if the recipient is not prepared and ready. Thus, strengthening the capacity of the prisoner is a top priority. These capabilities are considered to include improving the availability of high-quality, reliable, and granular data, as specified in the 17.18 target, and strengthening the statistical capability, as specified in the 17.19 target. In particular, in the era of artificial intelligence (AI) big data, global polarization is increasing in this area, and international cooperation to reduce the gap in this area is considered an urgent task.

2.4 The trade cooperation sector

This sector supports the establishment of an open, non-discriminatory, and equitable multilateral trade system based on global principles under the WTO system, while aiming to strengthen cooperation by expanding the export volumes of developing countries and applying preferential rules of origin.

In other words, the UN has recognized the importance of an open, equitable, non-discriminatory and predictable multilateral trading system consistent with the SDGs, while simultaneously supporting developing countries, so as to double the poorest countries' share in global exports. The UN aims to expand exports, achieve permanent tariff-free and quota-free market access for the least developed countries, and urge the implementation of simple and transparent rules of origin for goods from the least developed countries.

However, despite the efforts of the UN and the WTO, obstacles such as non-tariff barriers and supply constraints that do not comply with WTO rules and obligations remain, and the suggestion of trade consideration for or cooperation with developing countries has not been well observed amid the fierce struggle for leadership, as seen in the U.S.–China trade war.

2.5 Other institutional sectors

Other institutional aspects respect individual countries' policies and leadership in improving global macroeconomic safety, maintaining policy consistency, establishing and implementing policies, and further expanding and promoting effective public, private, and civil society partnerships to achieve goals.

First, strengthening global macroeconomic stability confirms the need for policy cooperation amongst countries to create a healthy economic environment in response to the global economic employment crisis and emphasizes the recommendation that countries pursue policy consistency to resolve macroeconomic imbalances. At the same time, the aid policies of developed countries are maintained as consistent with non-aid policies such as trade, investment, and agriculture, and policy consistency between government ministries is also required to help developing countries. It also specifies each country's policy discretion and leadership in policy establishment and implementation, which guarantees policy discretion due to concerns that the deepening interdependence of each country's economy and the emergence of rule-based systems violate countries' sovereignty.

Although this sector is also very important in terms of the basic conditions for global cooperation, maintaining the stability and policy consistency of the global macroeconomic economy while acknowledging each country's policy discretion and leadership is a reality in confrontations between East and West camps and struggles for leadership amongst the great powers. It is not an easy problem to solve, and the establishment of an omni-directional cooperation system incorporating public, private, and civil society seems like a distant future due to political and cultural differences.

3. Some suggestions for expanding global partnerships

Although SDG 17 comprises various detailed goals to revitalize global partnerships, with the intention of achievement by 2030, the following points need to be supplemented.

First, although the SDG implementation status check is subdivided into 17 areas to obtain indexes, SDG 17 lists 19 detailed goals. Thus, it is unsystematic and contains a lot of overlap. It is necessary to reorganize the target system into a more systematic framework in a more MECE (Mutualy Exclusive Collectively Exhaustive) manner. Although there is a goal system, implementation is limited because of the unclear relationships between the subjects and specific action plans. Therefore, it is necessary to develop specific evaluation indicators for each detailed goal and examine how global partnerships are changing through regular evaluation.

Second, although the transfer of global technology is currently mainly in the form of commercial contracts. Nowaday is the age of copy-left and AI technologies that can have a profound impact on humans are being made into open systems. In this respect, it is necessary to ensure that global technological cooperation can be exchanged via an open system. In particular, in the era of AI big data, the gap due to information bias is likely to intensify polarization, so special policies are needed to lessen the global technology and information gaps.

Lastly, it is necessary to strengthen the global communication base for global partnerships. The root of all problems, both at home and abroad, arises from lack of communication. For a smooth partnership, open communication to facilitate information sharing and the expression of opinions is essential, and in a global partnership, lack of communication due to political and cultural barriers is serious. In particular, communication difficulties due to language barriers are formidable, and it is important to develop language translation technologies such as GPT-3 to provide a foundation for the free exchange of meanings anytime and anywhere.

4. Conclusion

Global partnerships to achieve the SDGs have become an unavoidable trend, and now, the key is determining how to set and practice global norms for each sector. It is no exaggeration to say that the success of a global partnership depends entirely on mutual trust. However, trust is not formed in a short period of time; rather, trust forms gradually through continuous efforts over a long period of time. In that sense, the global village has a common destiny, and member countries should first recognize each other as partners who need to co-exist. To do this, it is necessary to establish win-win relationships with each other because a relationship cannot be sustained through the one-sided giving or receiving of help. In this regard, to strengthen global partnerships, not only developed countries but also developing countries should make meaningful efforts, while simultaneously strengthening the global communication base that facilitates these efforts.